# unraveling

## A Woman's Search for Freedom
## and the Journey of Coming Home

### MARTA HOBBS

SOUL-LED LLC

ISBN 979-8-218-10229-6 (hardback)
ISBN 979-8-218-10228-9 (paperback)
ISBN 979-8-218-12666-7 (eBook)
ISBN 979-8-218-12667-4 (audio)

Front cover design by Caroline Designs
Front cover photo by Rachel Calvo
Back cover and interior design by Christina Thiele
Edited by Anna Zweede and Brianne Bardusch

First Edition: February 2023

Published by Marta Hobbs and Soul-Led LLC
www.MartaHobbs.com

*To Mira and AJ,*
*I love you the most.*
*Thank you for the gift of being your mama.*

For you, the one holding this book, not knowing what to do next.

You are not alone. Healing is possible. As is freedom and
your best life yet.

It is never too late. You aren't broken. There's nothing
wrong with you.

You just forgot how sacred and loved you are.

I hope this story helps you to remember and to come home -
to yourself.

The answers you're seeking are all within.

Slow down and connect to your heart.

Breathe and tune into your soul.

Let me show you the way …

#  Contents:

## A Map for the Journey

### EXTERNAL JOURNEY – Part One

| | |
|---|---|
| Chapter 1 – The End | 3 |
| Chapter 2 – Running Away from Home | 11 |
| Chapter 3 – Stuck in Purgatory | 37 |
| Chapter 4 – Land of the Free | 45 |
| Chapter 5 – Movin' On Up | 75 |
| Chapter 6 – Fitting In, but Not Belonging | 89 |

### EXTERNAL JOURNEY – Part Two

| | |
|---|---|
| Chapter 7 – The American Dream | 111 |
| Chapter 8 – The Perfect Life | 155 |

### INNER JOURNEY

| | |
|---|---|
| Chapter 9 – The Unraveling | 179 |
| Chapter 10 – Healing Trauma | 195 |
| Chapter 11 – Finding Freedom | 217 |
| Chapter 12 – SoulCare Practice | 237 |
| Acknowledgments | 245 |
| About the Author | 251 |

*to un·rav·el*

- to cause to come apart as if by separating the threads of; to undo, to disentangle, to disengage

- to resolve the intricacy, complexity, or obscurity of; to clear up; to investigate and explain something complicated or puzzling

- to slowly start losing your mind and/or slowly start to go crazy

# External Journey

## PART ONE

# CHAPTER 1

## The End

was dying. I was dying and I was certain of it.

I felt it in my body. I knew it in my mind. I sensed it in my heart—the way it was beating—racing, pumping, painfully and rapidly pressing hard against my chest. It felt like at any moment it would violently break open, explode, or simply come to a sudden stop—and it would all be over—like I had wished for, but simultaneously feared, so many times before. It was hard to breathe and I felt like I was suffocating as tears streamed down my face and everything was spinning around and inside of me. My fingers and hands were going numb; my feet were tingly; my stomach felt like someone had punched me; my vision was blurry. My balance was off and I couldn't stand up straight—it felt like I had developed sea legs suddenly, that sensation you experience after having been on a cruise ship for a while. My whole body was shaking, pulsating, vibrating, and I couldn't put words together to form a sentence. My teeth rattled, my chin shook, and all I could do was sob, moan, and drip snot all over the shirt I was wearing. I was in the backseat of a car, in the middle of the pitch-black night, racing to the emergency room of the local hospital, the only hospital on the island. We were in St. Barths, a small island in the Caribbean.

Clinging with one hand to my husband's wrist, I held my other hand on top of my chest. Slumped over, leaning forward under the weight of all the pain that I was feeling, I looked out the window and felt the warm breeze come in from the outside and gently caress my skin. I stared up at the sky—the clear, dark, midnight sky filled with countless shimmering stars. They shone and sparkled like diamonds. It was beautiful. Magical. I saw the moon, keeping me company, following us on our way down the unpaved, narrow, curvy road. Then the magic evaporated. No street lamps. Just darkness. Darkness, hurry, and fear. I asked the moon, "Why? Why now? Why me? Why are you taking me?" and at the same time started frantically reciting "Our Father" and "Hail Mary" under my breath over and over in Polish, my mother tongue. My dad was driving, the passenger seat next to him empty. My mom stayed back with the kids, who didn't know what was happening. Jim and I sat in the back of the rented car, filled with sand from our time at the beach earlier in the week, holding on to each other, both scared shitless.

I managed to look over at him and whisper, "I need you to take care of the kids." I leaned against him, speaking into his ear, hyperventilating between each word. The moment the sentence left my mouth, I began sobbing uncontrollably again. Fear. Grief. Shock at the unfairness. My life was not finished! It was just too soon for it to end. I was devastated that I wouldn't get to see my children grow up. My crying continued, intensifying.

The ringing in my ears was like a freight train coming right at me, or the sound the locals say a hurricane makes when its center is hitting the island. It was deafening. The pain and darkness swallowed me whole and I was lost in the intensity of the combined physical sensations, incapable of thinking or reasoning. The only thing my brain could register was sheer panic and terror, with shrill alarms going off that I was in massive danger. I desperately wanted it to end.

My face felt like it was on fire and my head was pounding.

I was hysterical, unable to catch my breath, the unending waterfalls of tears soaking my clothes. I was sweating profusely.

Agony.

Things were getting fuzzy and dark before my eyes and the spins and dizziness grew unbearable. Everything started to sound and look like it was in slow motion, except the flashes of anger that detonated inside my head.

*This is so unfair!*

*How much more must I endure?! How much more must I suffer?!*

*Why has my life been so hard?*

And then, again, *Why me?! Why now?!*

---

At last we got to the hospital. I had to point out to my dad and my husband how to get in, where the front door was, my right hand hanging on to Jim's neck and my left on my father's shoulders, as they lifted and pulled me along. I struggled to keep myself upright. Once inside, I explained what was happening, speaking broken French through my tears and jittering teeth. The storm inside of me was still raging and felt like a heart attack and a seizure at the same time. Someone brought out a wheelchair and I gratefully collapsed into it as they pushed me forward.

In the painfully bright and overly air conditioned examination room, I was hooked up to all kinds of loud equipment. I let my father and husband tell my story and describe my situation to a doctor who came in. Thankfully, he was fluent in English and, I still noticed despite everything, also perfectly tanned. I threw up into a bucket and waited for everything to turn pitch black and my life to end.

Slowly, as the medication began kicking in, the horrible sensations diminished. My ears stopped ringing, the dizziness and nausea lessened, my vision cleared. My breathing was still uneven, but my body was no longer shaking and the unending tears had dried up. Becoming aware of this surprised me. I heard them say they would keep me overnight and realized we would not be flying back home the next day as planned.

I was wheeled into a private hospital room and helped into bed.

"What just happened?" I asked myself aloud when I was left alone. "How did it come to this?"

———————

We arrived on my favorite Caribbean island ten days earlier, I recalled. I had rented a dream villa for our family, both AJ and Mira were allowed to bring a friend on the trip and my parents had flown in to join us. We spent our days reading in the sun on pristine white-sand beaches while sipping pink champagne, evenings enjoying gourmet meals, laughter and love filling the space all around. A fancy and fabulous family vacation, just as I had imagined and planned. Everything I could wish for and more. Truly, a time in paradise …

Then what had made it all fall apart? Why had I started feeling so awful after our last dinner? We had just finished an incredible feast: lamb chops I cooked the perfect way, medium rare like I had learned in Paris, served with green beans, mashed potatoes, and our favorite red wine, Saint Emélion. It was a beautiful evening. *What went wrong?* I kept wondering, trying to figure it out, to solve this mystery somehow. It simply made no sense. *How could this even be possible?* The thoughts and questions trailed off as I drifted into a deep chemically induced slumber.

I woke up the following morning in a warm, sunny, white hospital room. It took me a moment to get my bearings as a nurse came in with breakfast. A fresh French croissant, orange juice, black coffee—perfection. This was Saint Barths after all, the playground of the rich and famous. Even the hospital service was fabulous.

The woman I was just twenty-four hours earlier—the successful, strong, well-put-together business owner, entrepreneur, mother, wife, and daughter—had vanished. In her place was someone I didn't recognize: a little girl somehow awakened for the first time, petrified of her surroundings and terrified by something inside herself as well. I desperately wanted someone to scoop me up and tell me that everything would be okay, that they would fix this and make my life sparkly and fabulous again. I wanted to go home, crawl into my bed, and sleep all this off. Or better yet, wake up to learn that it was all one long nightmare. I refused to admit that this was a crack in my beautifully polished surface created by pressure from within. And I didn't know things were only going to get much worse.

Back in Paris, for the next six months, I lived in this space of "dying" daily, the St. Barths episode playing over and over again (sometimes multiple times a day), endless panic attacks and constant anxiety. I was diagnosed with a serious heart condition and put on heavy medication in addition to the anti-anxiety pills. I was a wreck.

I was thirty-nine years old and I regularly found myself faced with paralyzing terror, unable to function normally. Some days I couldn't get out of bed; other times I had to leave things like dinner out or church service early because a panic attack came on. I mustered up enough energy to send the kids to school each morning and then suffered through the day until they returned in the afternoon. It took medicine to get me together enough to be available and present with them. Still, in the evening I was tortured by fear swooping in, barely able to make it through the family dinner I cooked, going upstairs to cry myself to sleep, and trying to hide this from my loved ones.

I was ashamed, embarrassed, and guilty about all of it. Everything, and also most people, told me that someone like me who had so much to be thankful for really had no reason to feel this way. It just made absolutely no sense. After all, I had finally gotten everything I ever wanted in life. I was happily married to the love of my life of 18 years. We had two children whom I adored, both of us loving them more than anything in the world, Mira who was 16 and 11-year-old AJ. I had built a company with Jim, which was incredibly successful and allowed us to be financially secure and then even retire when we sold it just six months prior. We had made the family decision to move to Paris, France, and each of us was thriving and enjoying our new city. I loved our home and our social life. We were part of an incredible community of people from all over the world at the American Church in Paris and the kids' international schools. I finally felt at home. I simply adored my life. I felt like I had finally arrived at the place toward which I had been steering all along. *I made it!* I thought, and I had big expectations of all the extraordinary things I was going to be doing here and now. I was a warrior, and all the working hard, achieving, pushing, accomplishing and being responsible, successful, strong, and tough brought me just where I had dreamed of being. It was even better than I imagined! And now that I could finally take a breath from all the years of hard work and striving, this was no time for a breakdown! This was not in my plans whatsoever.

My ideal life, and what I thought was the best version of myself, broke apart in St. Barths, and then in Paris, the unraveling began. All the balls I was juggling dropped out of my hands and hit the ground, shattering. The race I had been running came to a sudden forced pause and I simply fell apart, coming completely unglued. I suddenly realized how exhausted and lonely I felt keeping it all together all these years. In the City of Light, a place where life had seemed like a dream come true, my dark childhood trauma showed up on the scene as I began the search for healing.

It did not feel like a search, much less like healing, at the time.

It felt like torture. And terror.

I did not want any of it. I wasn't ready or even slightly interested. I did not welcome nor appreciate the interruption. I often tried to escape it, resist it, or hide from it and hoped for life to get back to normal.

But it was impossible.

This journey would take me straight into the center of my pain and suffering. It was, I know now, a sacred doorway, and the first step toward unchaining myself from the weight of the wounds of my past, which had been holding me captive. At last, in Paris, twenty-seven years after escaping from Communist oppression and fleeing my homeland as a child, I asked myself the question, "What does freedom mean *to me?*"

The first step to finding an answer was revisiting my childhood in Poland.

This started my journey within.

CHAPTER 2

# Running Away From Home

## SZCZECIN, POLAND

### 1974–1987

Empty shelves. No food in the markets and a lack of supplies in the grocery stores. Lines formed when a shop had goods available, and someone would call my parents to tell them to send my younger sister and me to stand in line. We would hold the spot and Mamuś (Mommy) or Papuś (Daddy) would come with the coupons issued by the government which allowed us a certain amount of the day's treasure, and with money to pay for it. Rations, I think the coupons were called. Everything was very controlled and very limited. Sometimes we stood in line for fresh rolls, sometimes it was sausage or cheese, one time it was pantyhose and even a bathing suit with palm trees on it. It was brown and orange like the sunset and it didn't fit—we bought it for when it would. The waiting was usually several hours, and the lines were normally stretched around the block. The worst feeling was when whatever we were waiting for ran out before it was our turn to buy it. We left disappointed on those days, after hearing someone up front shout "there is no more!" to the people in the back.

I was never really hungry, but there was a pervasive sense of scarcity, and some days for supper we only ate stale bread with butter and sugar on top and drank tea. Fresh bread was rare. If we got word, on the weekend, that there would be some, we had to stand in a very long line for it. Asking how old the loaf was, to know what you were getting, was important. If it was more than three days old, we wouldn't buy it because it was inedible. Warm rolls were a decadent treat and one of my favorites.

All of the buildings, the sidewalks, the streets, were a dull gray. The clothes of the people outside too. All of it was gray, and it smelled of sadness. Secretly, I longed for color, beauty, and adventure. My wishes were rarely granted, but I was fortunate, because sometimes they were.

The neighborhood kids called my family "rich," which embarrassed me. We had a color TV at a time when other people had only a black-and-white set, if they had one at all. We also owned a car, which was not just a Fiat or a Škoda but French. An unheard of luxury! It was one my dad put together on one of his excursions to junk yards in foreign countries to earn extra money, but the kids didn't know that. They just saw a shiny, awesome Citroën pulling up in the courtyard of our apartment building and often wanted to go for a ride in it. My dad, more often than not, proudly accommodated their requests.

Being "rich" also meant that we got to travel places in our "fancy" car over the summer. We came back with rare things like colored markers, a new backpack, a pair of shoes for the year, and even maybe a new toy. Most of our friends never left the country and had no access to colorful new clothes or cool toys or foreign candy. We all wore hand-me-downs (or things that we'd eventually "grow into" that were too big) and one pair of shoes until they had holes in them or feet could no longer squeeze inside.

When we came back from a trip, my younger sister Ania and I shared candy with our neighborhood friends. They stood around us in a tight circle, eyes wide in amazement, holding out their cupped hands. We handed each one a piece of candy wrapped in colorful paper or shiny, sparkly foils, gummy bears, and little Coca Cola–shaped sweets.

"Give me one! Give me one!" they clamored.

It was hard when someone wanted a second, because this was treasure and it had to last for a while. Our trips to fancy foreign lands only happened once a year.

"Sorry, we can't," the two of us told them. It made me feel bad inside.

We showed them other things they hadn't seen before, exciting things from "across the border." Cool puffy stickers that smelled nice when you rubbed them and colorful, shiny hair accessories. In Szczecin, we could only get beige rubber bands and black bobby pins. Ania and I were terribly proud to tie our pigtails with bright elastics, and wear hair clips with ribbons or tiny bears or flowers on them. But the wonder of all wonders was a very special pencil case we brought back from West Berlin. It was red and it had three colorful teddy bears on it. I held it up ceremoniously with one hand and slowly opened the zipper that ran around three of the four sides, holding my breath, then sighed in delight. A row of brightly colored pencils, all neatly lined up, the pencil sharpener in its special spot, a small matching ruler—and then my favorite—a fountain pen! This, too, was treasure, and used very sparingly for school projects only. Ania and I both got to pick out a new one each summer, for the first day of classes, along with colorful backpacks and decorative notebooks. I loved school because of this, my sparkly, new supplies.

The summer vacation trips were my favorite times. I got to leave the grayness and enter a world of sunshine, bright lights, and lots of colors for a while. It was magical. Running free on a beach somewhere in Greece, living in a tiny camper with my family, eating grapes straight off the vines and watching my skin turn brown and my hair become blonde, I loved all of it. Szczecin and restrictions and monotony were forgotten. I didn't care that it took us a whole week of driving and sleeping on the sides of the roads and in parking lots. On each of those summer trips, I became a creature I loved, the tanned girl who ran wild in nature with wind in her hair, sand between her toes, the taste of salt on her lips, and the sound of the ocean surrounding her. I was carefree, always laughing, liberated from the pain and sorrow I accumulated in my body during the rest of the year.

The other connection we had to the world beyond Polish borders came from my dad. He worked at our local TV station as a camera operator and lighting director, but for extra money he fixed cars in junkyards with his friends in West Germany. This was completely illegal of course. He took the risk happily, because tinkering with cars was his passion and love. It was never primarily about the extra cash for him. When Papuś came back from Germany, he brought candy and bananas. Ania and I would be in heaven! Once he snuck across the border to France (without the required visa or passport, naturally) and came back with sweet green grapes, fabulous French cheese, and exciting stories. It felt so fancy, and it was, compared to normalcy. I felt fully alive and vibrant in those moments.

The other high points of the year were Christmas and Easter. On those holidays, I was surrounded by people who loved me. There were big family get-togethers, the kind where we had to borrow chairs from the neighbors because we didn't have enough seats in our apartment for everyone. It was festive and so much fun. The house was filled with love and laughter. I loved helping my mom prepare for the big events and then getting to be the hostess along with her. My favorite thing to do was to help bake the cheesecake. Every special occasion had traditional Polish cheesecake. Some people added raisins and nuts inside. We only added raisins. They had to soak in hot water before we added them to the batter so that they would not sink to the bottom of the cake, but stay spread throughout. I loved mixing it (by hand, of course, with a giant wooden spoon) and measuring out the ingredients to add in. The best part of the process was getting to lick the bowl clean, after the batter was poured into a baking dish and placed in the oven. The kitchen and then the whole house started to smell amazing. Mamuś and Papuś cooked whatever main course we were serving together. My biggest job, besides the cheesecake, was setting the table. One of my parents would iron the tablecloth and place it on the table (or spread it across several tables if we had that many guests). Then Ania and I were to place napkins, plates, silverware, and glasses on the table. Everything went in a certain order: knives on the right of the plate, forks on the left, dessert spoons on top of the plate. Once I got older I could also help by chopping vegetables for salads and side dishes, and then I watched my dad create special decorations to go on top. He would make silly faces using tomatoes, carrots, and parsley so that the salads would look like they were smiling. Each dish had to have serving spoons. That was our job too.

For these occasions, Mamuś made us skirts or dresses from pretty fabrics my dad picked up in Germany. What my mother sewed for us was all the more precious to Ania and me because nothing like it was available in Polish stores. The clothes made me feel like a princess. I felt beautiful. Getting dressed always took place after the table was set and the food was nearly ready. We would put on our freshly ironed skirts or dresses and then wait for people to start ringing the doorbell. This was the most exciting part: getting to greet our family and friends, taking their coats (they always got piled on top of my parents' bed because we didn't have enough closet space or hangers), receiving the flowers guests brought for the house, and hearing them say, "Oh, look at you! You look so pretty!" I loved those dinner parties. Especially the dancing that would go late into the night, once the meal was finished and tea or coffee and cheesecake were served. Music and laughter filled the space and we got to stay up super late with the grown-ups.

My mom was a journalist and a reporter for a nightly live evening news show at the same TV station where my dad was employed. Everyone knew her in town—she was a well-known and much-beloved celebrity—and so everyone also knew my sister and me. This was helpful when store owners held things for us under the counter or we could get into a sold-out show at the kids' theater or attend Christmas parties at the TV station where there were presents and dancing. And when the Chernobyl nuclear power plant exploded in the neighboring Ukraine, and all the kids thought we were going to die when the black nuclear death cloud finally reached us, we were some of the few that got to have those scary injections in shady offices of special doctors ensuring that we wouldn't die after all.

However, Mom's fame also came at a very high price.

She refused to join the Communist party as was required of members of the press at the time, and became very active in the Solidarity movement. She was declared anti-government and considered a political threat. She had opinions and dreams of justice and freedom—she had traveled the world and seen "the West." Her father before her fought in World War II for the liberation of his country and she was determined to carry that torch. What this meant for me, before it became more, was living in the constant threat of danger.

My sister and I both knew that our phone line was tapped and our family was followed; we understood that police could come barging through the front door at any moment. And when they did, the raids we witnessed inside our home were alarming. Ania and I sat on the couch of our living room. My knees were pulled up to my chin, my heart raced, and my eyes were wide with shock. The policemen were stern; their voices strong and loud. They spoke in short, direct sentences and asked questions. They rummaged through the coffee table drawers. I wasn't sure if they were looking for something in particular. My parents yelled at them, and they yelled back. I sensed danger, felt like I was in trouble, and longed for it to end, staying quiet, as expected. These men who represented the country's government so violently going through our home and our things. *That's how the world works*, I thought. *Even the people who are supposed to keep us safe are against us.*

It was scary, and it was also incomprehensible. The things they took were silly in my opinion: foreign newspapers or magazines, bootlegged copies of American movies. They took anything from other countries. "Western Propaganda!" they called it. We had *Rambo* (dubbed in Polish), which I loved watching. It was somehow a threat to the Polish government—even on a VCR tape—and was confiscated.

My sister and I were instructed never to open the front door if someone knocked, to ask "Who is it?" and then only unlock the door when it was Grandpa. No one else was safe. Once I innocently opened up the door after a knock, excited to see who was coming to visit and it was the police, the "bad" police. I felt like the raid was my fault and I was terrified by the stress I caused my parents while it was happening. So from then on, if we suspected anything strange, we were supposed to say "Nobody's home!" through the closed door. We would wait, hardly breathing, listening, looking at each other, until the men on the other side of the door left. When I got tall enough to see through the peephole in the door, it made life a bit easier. Easier because I could see when it actually was my grandpa, but still terrifying. Panic rose inside of me each time the doorbell rang. It was hard to sometimes tell the difference between the excitement over guests coming or the fear of the policemen knocking. Both felt like a sharp jolt of energy rushing through my body. I got accustomed to it being there.

Two men often waited in the stairwell of our apartment building, usually smoking and speaking in hushed tones, and we knew they were there for us. They were watching who was coming and going. I was used to looking out my window and seeing someone standing there too, across the busy street we lived on, pretending to read the newspaper but keeping tabs on the movements in and out of our house.

This was what being home was like, a sort of prison with guards around it. But although I was often frightened, I thought all of it was normal because that's just how it was.

Outside, danger was always looming over me or waiting around the next corner. I knew that from my own experience and my parents' directives. I loved playing outside with my friends but I always had to keep an eye out for anything suspicious. It made losing myself in play as a little girl impossible. I had to try to stay a step ahead of any possible danger, expecting it to come at me any moment and be prepared. So I was always on guard, scanning my environment for where the next attack would come from, trying to predict it so that I could ensure my survival. And then I had to make sure Ania was okay too. One eye out for danger—second eye on my little sister.

Nonetheless, I loved to play with my friends, even if I had to keep looking over my shoulder. I loved riding our bikes in a group around our neighborhood in the city. I loved roller skating, playing games with our jump ropes, running to the playground nearby and swinging on swings for hours while singing. At home, I loved coloring, drawing, playing with LEGOs or dressing up our dolls, dancing, singing and just being silly. But my favorite was playing "pretend". Ania and I dressed in our parents' clothes and became fancy ladies going fabulous places. Since we didn't have purses, I placed a string on my shoulder and then hung a book on it by its spine. I did the same for my sister. It looked the part, but of course you could never place anything inside. It was good enough. We made train tickets and went on trips, lining up chairs like inside of a train car and, after validating our tickets, we explored beautiful destinations and spoke fake foreign languages. Playing "pretend" outside with a larger group usually meant we had a secret mission to complete. We became international spies or land explorers or good guys getting away from the bad, our imaginations running wild. I spent a lot of time up in my head envisioning all kinds of wonderful things and adventures. It was my favorite way to escape when things got too scary. I liked hanging out there. It felt safe.

On weekdays after school, we were always accompanied by our nanny, Ciocia Andzia. Old enough to be our grandma, she loved us as if we were her own and kept a close eye on us when we played outside. She sat on a bench nearby and anytime someone was even a little bit mean or threatening, she had no qualms about walking over and stepping in.

"Hey, you!" she yelled to the troublemakers, "Go away!"

She waved her arm dismissing them at the same time and that was that. The bad kids always ran. They called her "baba jaga" – a witch.

Sometimes in the evenings, when our parents attended dinners, parties, or late meetings, Ania and I were left alone at home. We watched *Tom and Jerry* on VCR tape on loop and stayed up late. It was exciting but terrifying being responsible for us both, but I did my best to be brave. The staying up late part was exciting, but I always hoped Mom and Dad would return before it was time for sleeping. Because sometimes at bedtime, with the lights out and no noise from the TV, my sister would get very scared and start crying.

"Marta?" Ania whispered from the bed across the room once the lights were out. "Marta, I can't fall asleep."

I could hear her sniffling.

"Think about something which makes you happy," I responded,

"like your favorite thing. Think about that. And then when you fall asleep, you can dream about it. Make it something really good. I think about riding my bike in the park. Try it."

A few minutes later, I heard her again.

"Marta? Marta, I'm afraid."

"Okay, you can come here. But let's play a game. Let's pretend that the space between our two beds is an ocean. The carpet? It's the ocean, okay? And you have to run really really fast to me because there are sharks swimming in the ocean and you don't want them to eat you, okay? I'm gonna count three-two-one and then you go. Ready?"

I don't know why I thought I needed to add a little bit of extra fear to let her sleep in my single-person bed with me. But I did. She raced the ten or so feet between our beds while I screamed for her to "Hurry up!" It was such a relief when she made it, which was, of course, *every* time.

She would snuggle up with me and calm down. But on certain occasions her crying was so intense that not only could I not soothe her, I had trouble keeping myself together. On those nights, we lay there together crying out for Mom, completely hysterical, knowing deep down inside that nobody was coming to save us.

When I got old enough to use the phone, my parents would leave a phone number to call in case of emergencies. We would sometimes call and ask when they were coming home … When they got back they would explain that it was all so silly because there wasn't anything to fear. Which I knew wasn't really true. Life showed me proof otherwise. So I had two very strong forces running through me for as far back as I can remember, being afraid but also being brave: terror and courage.

I became Ania's protector. This made me feel grown up, and responsible. It also earned me praise from my parents, so not only did I feel like I was helping, I also felt nice to hear I was being a "good girl." While taking care of my little sister was something expected of me, it was also completely natural. I was older. I was taller. I was more mature. Perhaps I also had a little bit of extra experience with fear, and taking on a role of helping Ania with her own was a welcome relief from having to sit with mine. When she was too scared in preschool and the teachers couldn't get her to stop crying, they would get me out of kindergarten to come soothe her. They didn't call my mom—maybe she was too busy or too important or too famous. They came and got me instead. One time this got me out of mandatory naptime, which I hated, so I was actually grateful for the responsibility sometimes.

Ania went through a period of unpredictable fainting spells for a while. We would be sitting at the supper table and she'd suddenly fall off her chair passing out, to the right or to the left. Most times my dad somehow managed to catch her midfall and she never hit the floor. Once, however, she did just that. Falling face first in the bathroom while standing. I was taking a bath and my mom was in the bathroom brushing Ania's wet hair. She had just finished taking her bath. Suddenly Ania fell forward, landing in between the bathroom sink and the washing machine. My mom and I were screaming and my dad came running. We lifted her, laid her out on my parents' bed, and she came to. I don't know if they ever got to the bottom of what was going on, but I remember my sister being scared a lot when she was little, scared a lot and crying quite a bit. It frightened me and then it also annoyed me because it added to the already chaotic atmosphere and drama. Now there was more. It was a lot for a kid. For me, and for her too. We just each dealt with it differently. I kept it all inside feeling lonely and isolated. She let it out by crying. The fuss made me uncomfortable because I just wanted her to be okay.

One of the happiest days of my life, and also somewhat of a solution to the scary nights and frequent fear, was when we got a family dog. He was a black-and-white German short-haired pointer whom we named Mores. When he arrived in our house, he was just a puppy of a few weeks and I was in love from the moment we picked him up. I wasn't prepared for how much he cried the first few nights in our apartment. When my parents explained that he was crying for his mommy because he wasn't used to being all alone, my heart nearly split in two. I snuck him into my bed at night after everyone else had fallen asleep. I'd pet and kiss him whispering that it was okay; he was safe. I actually spoke those words to the both of us, comforting myself while I soothed Mores. The cuddles and licks from my new four-legged best friend helped a lot too.

Growing up constantly surrounded by fear meant watching the TV news and listening to the radio for the latest Solidarity protest, Lech Wałęsa's controversial speeches from shipyards on strike, and attempts of the government to silence and put all those down. This was the birthing time of a brand-new revolt of the Polish people against Communism, still in power over our country. Poland, at the time, was under the Soviet Union's influence and Solidarity was a trade union that started the anti-Communist movement with Wałęsa as its leader. The Polish Communist government was doing its best to destroy the union, the Solidarity movement, and all those with ties to it, which meant civil unrest, country-wide strikes, tanks in the streets to contain them, censorship, political repression, economic depression, high prices and lack of supplies of any kind in the stores, massive job layoffs. And amid all this, it was Polish people fighting against Polish people—on their own land—a war among sisters and brothers; a family divided. This was the backdrop for my childhood, the final years of the Cold War.

Learning about people who were kidnapped, gone missing, and sometimes turning up murdered in a trunk of a car (like a famous Catholic priest who also supported Solidarity and the people's freedom) was common. Hearing the leaders in our government issue orders for countrywide curfews or martial law was normal. The adults would gather silent and tense (usually with vodka and cigarettes) and shush the kids so they could hear every word spoken and then respond with shock or anger at what was being communicated. I grew up watching buildings get burned down, police beating those who wanted things to be fair and just, and a constant feeling of stress, secrecy, and conspiracy theories. And it wasn't from movies or books or stories—it was my life and my experience of being a kid. Danger. Threat. Unrest. If we had moments when we forgot the nature of our reality, the songs we listened to and the children's shows we watched on TV would remind us, because most of what I watched were series about soldiers during a war, or adventures of kids during the Warsaw Uprising, or sole rebels fighting against an unjust government or power (who'd usually end up dead). *Tom and Jerry* came from the West (snuck in on a bootlegged VCR tape from Germany) and that was a most-welcome departure from the home-produced kid shows, also controlled by Communist propaganda. I must not forget my beloved *Little House on the Prairie* and *Lassie*, both dubbed into Polish by the same monotone, emotionless, male narrator—that was allowed. One show was the representation of what girls my age must be like in America; the other made me cry every single time a dog, the show's hero, saved someone's life. But that wasn't the real world. Reality was that war was in my very bones, not just echoing through the culture but in my DNA.

Both of my parents were "World War II Babies" (Mamuś was born shortly after the war ended and Papuś right in the middle of it) while my grandparents fought in the war themselves. My dad's parents were shot during WWII while he was just two years old. They hid Jews in their barn, keeping them from being sent to the Holocaust by the Nazis. They were discovered and executed in that very barn. My dad grew up as an orphan raised by his aunt and uncle and taken in by their family. My mom's mother survived the war but died when my mom was only eighteen.

My only living grandparent, my grandpa on mom's side, was a famous colonel in the war. He survived not only war, the uprising and many battles and combats (getting shot in the chest during a battle in Warsaw, a money clip with bills in his pocket saving his life!) but also a wrongful lifelong prison sentence, which was reversed after he served eight years. The celebration of his release was short-lived. My grandmother died and my mom was left with her older brother and dad, who worked tirelessly for the freedom and betterment of the country he served, even after he was put in prison. He was probably a tough father for a daughter to have but he was an incredible grandpa. He was the one person who made me feel safe. He was tall and big and I remember his giant hands and hugs and kisses and a lot of time spent sitting in his lap while he read stories. He didn't just read them—he recited them passionately in his deep and powerful voice! We called him by his Warsaw Uprising pseudonym, Ziuk, and he often talked about his favorite cavalry horse and going into battle against the Germans and Russians in the resistance, World War II, or the Warsaw Uprising. Maybe that's what made him so powerful to me—his stories of war and survival made me feel protected in his presence. I saw swords and numerous medals on display in his study and photos of him in uniform (which he still wore while speaking in public). This somehow symbolized to me that I had someone on my side who could defend me. With all this in my blood, I was practically born in a warrior's stance—fists clenched, chest out, feet firmly on the ground, ready for battle—revolution running through my veins.

Even our annual summer trips away included fear to start, because before getting to paradise, we had to cross the border to get out of Poland and there was always a chance we would not be allowed to leave on the Polish side. Then there was the stress of crossing the German border because we might not be allowed to enter. All the right paperwork had to be presented and be in order: visas, stamps, signatures, passports, permissions, you name it. Thus, all vacations started with hours of sitting in our car in long lines of others in their cars hoping to simply get away. Sometimes it took so long that my mom would get out of the passenger seat and get into the trailer attached to our car and start making dinner. The border police would inspect every vehicle and diligently take apart several cars looking for cash that might be hidden in creative places (this was before the age of credit cards) and they were pretty motivated and thorough. If they found any money, they got to confiscate it. And what made it really scary was that we usually were indeed hiding cash somewhere in our car. It might be underneath the ashtray or behind the front head light or sewn into the seats. We wanted to buy things like bubble gum and fruit and fancy cheese, which we had no access to at home. I would hold my breath every time it was our turn to be inspected, watching the little mirror on wheels sliding under the bottom of our Citroën. And then again when the policemen looked over all of our travel documents, intensely staring into each of our faces with every passport photo. But eventually we'd make it out. I remember not being able to leave just once, and it was because our car wouldn't start after waiting in line for so long.

The fact that Papuś worked on cars meant that we were always traveling in some contraption that he had just "rescued" at his latest junkyard adventure, so breaking down on highways in foreign countries became a common part of our family holidays. And foreign countries meant foreign languages. Polish isn't exactly universal and we did not speak English back then—and neither did the people we encountered in the countryside of Romania, Bulgaria, or Yugoslavia—but we managed with the international language of mimicking and the universal communication skills of pointing to things (mainly the broken parts of the car engine my dad was trying to rebuild with the spare parts in the trunk).

During these breaking-down times of our family trips, we would just stop and pull over wherever we were and set up camp as my dad opened up the hood of the car and went at it. Our camper-trailer was really too small for four people with a large dog and too low for even one adult person to stand upright in. But that became home. We never stayed in hotels because we could not afford them. My mom would turn on the radio, tune in to a local station for music, get out the camping stove, and start boiling water and peeling potatoes. If we happened to break down next to a cornfield, we would be having corn that day. If we stopped by a forest, we would go pick mushrooms to cook. One time this led to a whole week of food poisoning by mushrooms that were apparently not supposed to be eaten. But sometimes good things would happen: a truck would pass by and drop a few watermelons on the road or we'd be stopped somewhere with grapes or figs or maybe even a place to walk to that had a bathroom and a shower. My parents called these times "an adventure," and somehow I picked up on the idea that they were supposed to be fun. It was a fine line between stressful and fun, but I ignored my anxiety and made myself useful by trying to assist my dad in fixing the car or helping my mom prepare the food.

---

Eventually, when I was ten, my mother was terminated from her high-profile TV job and blacklisted as a journalist, which meant she could not legally work in the country. She was fired because she refused to join the Communist party and thus, they could not control and censor what she might say on her nightly live newscast called "Kronika." Many people watched and loved her, and then, suddenly, she was off the air and disappeared in life too. She became a mark, and people associated with her became targets. She lost a lot of friends, besides losing her job, career, and life's direction at that time. Our home, which was usually noisy and filled with people talking and laughing, became empty and much more quiet and calm. Sadness filled the air. Depression. Confusion. Loss. It felt like life was suddenly sucked out of the place. Many whom my parents considered friends ran from them because they were afraid for their families, their own well-being and safety. My mom started writing for underground newspapers that secretly published anti-Communist content, while my dad kept his job at the TV station to earn money and pay the bills. The few guest visits that did take place during this time were always behind closed doors in the kitchen and involved hushed tones and a lot of cigarette smoke. Although my mom was home more than before, she didn't seem too happy about it. I remember her stress and sadness.

In order to help make ends meet, we picked up an extra job as a family delivering packages sent from the West to private homes in Szczecin. Local post offices couldn't be trusted with the content (items would get confiscated, stolen, or go missing) so private companies would show up with trucks and fill our small two-bedroom apartment with big cardboard boxes, which we then hand delivered to lucky residents of our city.

Several times, when Mores was still young, having boxes stacked up in the hallway next to his bed caused a big problem. He always hated to stay home alone. This was one of the many things we had in common! He would let us know just how much he hated it by getting into something and chewing it into pieces. The boxes gave him a new target besides the shoes he chewed on usually. We came home one evening after dinner at a relative's home to find expensive toilet paper, coffee beans, and colorful lollipops shredded and scattered all over our home. Another time he consumed a delivery of cookies and cakes, being quite selective with his choices. The mess was horrifying, and none of those items were available in stores to be replaced. It got even uglier because Mores got a beating as his punishment while my sister and I cried watching. Frankly, I didn't think this business venture was worth the trouble it caused.

Mores had this interesting habit of running away from home, which scared the living shit out of me. My parents had this interesting habit of letting him out by himself—out the apartment door he'd go, out of the building, no dog collar, no ID—and we lived in the center of a city with cars, trains, busses, and lots of traffic. Sometimes he'd come back and scratch at the apartment door to get back in. Other times we'd have to check to be sure if someone hadn't closed the building doors for him to get in and up the stairs. When he was nowhere to be found, my dad would stick his head out the window and whistle for the animal. And some days, he simply would choose his freedom. In one of those instances, he was missing for over 24 hours and I thought I had lost him forever. I was in third or fourth grade and went to school with a black-and-white picture of him and cried all day. I even failed a math test because I couldn't get my thoughts together. It didn't help that when I would manage to calm down, I'd stare at his photo again, and sob even harder. I didn't cry a lot when I was little so perhaps this was a way to let out some of what had built up over some time. Eventually, Mores came back and, while I was thrilled and wanted to hug and kiss him, my dad would whip him with his leather leash for running away in the first place. I hated it.

———

Not long after my mom's termination from the television station, our home was invaded in the middle of the night while we were all sleeping. I vaguely remember voices, and noise and commotion, and our bedroom door being closed shut. (I always insisted on sleeping with it open because I was afraid at night.) When I got up the next morning, my mother was gone. She never went away alone, so I knew something was wrong. While my sister and I were assured that Mom was just on a business trip to Warsaw, I noticed lots of funny stares, worried conversations, and whispering within our family circle over the next few days. Conspiracy, that had been in the air a lot already, ramped up to a new level. Everyone kept reassuring me, saying Mamuś would be back soon. I believed their words over what I felt in my gut and pretended that I wasn't as terrified as I really was. This meant my own body wasn't a safe place either, since my own feelings and emotions couldn't be trusted. They apparently sent the wrong signals about what was happening externally. Or so others told me.

In reality, I would later learn, my mother was kidnapped, imprisoned with other journalists and activists, and interrogated. For three days my father had no news at all, until someone recognized her and snuck out a note she scribbled on a tiny piece of lined paper. It said, "I am alive. Take care of the girls. I love you." I am pretty sure my parents did not know if Mom would survive this ordeal, nothing like a business trip to the country's capital. When she did finally return home, a decision was made to seek political asylum outside of Poland. I was twelve years old.

I remember the day my parents told us the news. We were all in the kitchen and my mom was combing my long hair. My parents asked my sister and me how we would feel about going to live in America.

I was excited. I loved when we drove through West Germany on our way to Greece and everything was so bright and colorful. I looked forward to the neon signs, colorful store displays, and people in bright clothes in the countries of Western Europe. I imagined America was even better, filled with flashing lights like New York City, which I had seen in the movies, and with McDonald's and people in jeans and country music everywhere. (My parents loved playing Elvis, Kenny Rogers and Dolly Parton on cassette tapes during those dinner parties and late-night dancing.) Everyone with big wide smiles and perfect teeth. It seemed so exotic, so wonderfully foreign and so far away. Surely there would be candy, fruit, toys, a large selection of clothes to choose from, and colorful markers and pretty notebooks for school. That's what the twelve-year-old me really wished for. That was freedom to me back then! I immediately began to imagine how life would be different, to dream that I wouldn't have to hear that I couldn't have those wonderful things because we couldn't afford them. Rather than just driving by and seeing those shiny objects once a year, on the summer drive through the capitalist Western Bloc countries, and dreaming of them and settling for the grayness, the fear, the sadness of life in Communist Poland. What might it feel like to just live among the beautiful things instead? To be surrounded by them, was that what it was like in America? A German friend of my parents told them once that they drank Coca Cola with milk there. He said he'd been to the United States. Although that cocktail sounded gross, I was looking forward to our new adventure. It would be like an amazing vacation to a cool place except that we would get to stay forever! This was what I always wanted on our summer driving trips to Greece—to not return.

My sister, who must have been around nine at the time, cried hysterically. When my parents asked her why she was sobbing, she said it was because she did not want to marry an American. I wonder what exactly an "American husband" represented to a little girl from Poland at that age.

We were both promised that our dog would come with us and that was the most crucial detail to us both. He'd stopped eating things from foreign packages at last, so he'd get to join us now that he was well behaved.

One thing about this special trip, however, was very important. We could not tell *anyone* that we were going. Not a single soul. The government would definitely try to detain us based on what was happening in the country at the time, so in order for the plan to succeed, we had to keep it to ourselves. A secret spy mission like in James Bond movies I had seen before. I was 007.

It was a little hard going to school after receiving that information. I was finishing sixth grade in the elementary school I had attended since kindergarten. A mixture of fear and excitement filled my heart and my belly when I thought about the big secret, but I had to say nothing and stay focused on my schoolwork and pretend that we were going to Italy for the summer. I had to contain and conceal all that energy inside of myself. My parents applied for visas to enter the country and we had the proper passport stamps and all the right paperwork to show on our exit and border crossings so it looked legit and we wouldn't get stopped while leaving. Italy was our family's cover story. So I walked around that June telling everyone at Szczecin's elementary school #63 that I was going to Rome and I would see them in September. I was lying.

In the weeks leading up to our departure, various strangers walked through our home purchasing random things. Not furniture, as that would have been too suspicious. We left all that behind. They came and bought china, vases, decorative objects— small things that could be carried out of the apartment without raising any red flags. A particular drapery of a sun that hung in the bedroom my sister and I shared was sold to a woman one day and I was devastated. My mom felt pretty bad about it and told me she would not have sold it if she knew it meant that much to me. But I wasn't really crying for the orange-and-red sun. I never really cared for it anyway; I thought it was ugly. I was thankful it hung above my sister's bed rather than mine. The tears were about being scared out of my mind, having to carry around this huge secret, and being forced to run away for my own safety and leaving behind life as I knew it. I was watching people pay insignificant amounts of money for the things that were everything to me. My home, my identity, my frame of reference for life, my world were all crumbling right in front of me. It was extremely frightening and disorienting, and there was nothing to hang on to, to stabilize myself. We were heading into the unknown. Polish citizens were not allowed to even visit the USA without a special invitation from an American citizen and a lengthy application process, which required in-person visits to the American embassy in Warsaw. Not a single person I knew had ever set foot in that country.

But I had to hide all my fears because I wasn't going to be the one who gave the secret away. We needed to be able to run away that summer. And I wasn't going to be a baby about it. So I wiped my tears, packed my LEGOs, and imagined my many new friends in fabulous dresses with curly blonde hair who were going to show me around and play with me. Maybe I'd even get a real Barbie doll! I had only had a fake one up until then, her name was Fleur. She had curly red hair and my mom often made clothes for her using leftover fabric from the dresses and skirts she made for Ania and me. I loved her, but she was not Barbie!

---

It was Mores who got out of Communist oppression first. There was no way the border police would buy the Italy story if we were leaving with our large dog, apparently. He was a German short-haired pointer (one of the first complicated things I learned to say in English after arriving in the USA) and weighed about a hundred pounds. Friends who lived in West Berlin took him ahead of time and snuck him out across the border. Saying goodbye to him was really hard and I cried for hours because I was afraid I would never get to see him again. My biggest fear was that I would not be reunited with my pup, and I was always afraid of something bad happening to him. It was all so scary and overwhelming, especially as it was getting closer to go time.

Besides not telling our friends and classmates, we also had to keep this "move" hidden from our whole family. It was somehow decided that two people would get to know, my mom's brother and my beloved grandpa, Dziadziu Ziuk. While I don't remember any details of packing, preparing, and driving away, I clearly remember the day we left him. We were in my grandpa's country home that summer for some time together before our goodbyes and departure, and he broke down when it was time for us to go. He sobbed loud and hard, his whole body shaking. I had never heard a human make a sound like that before. He could not utter a word—he was grieving our loss so very much. I thought my heart would break or explode or both. I could not catch my breath and the tears came so hard, so much, so fast, the silent kind. The ones that you want to scream with but you just can't, and so your mouth opens wide and everything hurts and there is no sound. Only pain. Deep, deep ache inside. And a river of tears. I remember driving away in the car with our things piled on top (no camper this time; we had sold that too) looking out the back window, and him standing there, leaning on his cane, hunched over by the weight of all the pain. He waved until he thought we were too far away to see him anymore, then he sat down and dropped his head into his palms. The man who fought in wars and battles and survived injuries, gunshot wounds, imprisonment, the death of the love of his life—this warrior now completely helpless and overtaken by tears and this latest (maybe the biggest) loss in his life. It hurt more than my own sadness and grief to witness him that way.

Did losing us, seeing us flee Poland, make him feel his life's work had been for nothing? His fight for freedom and willingness to give his life up for his country was not enough to bring freedom to his daughter and her family. Did he see this as a proclamation of failure, voiding all of his efforts?

He fought for liberation and stayed. His daughter fought for liberation but left. Did this feel like a failed mission somehow? I felt his pain and these questions very deeply.

I cannot imagine the rest of my family, the people we celebrated with every Christmas, Easter, and New Year's Eve. The ones who shared our baptisms, birthdays, first communions, national and school holidays. How did they find out? Did they call our home several times and not get an answer and worry? Did they wonder why we were not answering the door when they rang the doorbell? Did they look for our car outside our building and become curious why we hadn't come back from Italy? Were there rumors? Gossip? News? Were they afraid we were taken? Hurt? Was there perhaps a letter that got circulated later? And then once they somehow got the "official word" that we were gone for good, how deep the hurt must have been. How awful the betrayal of not being trusted with the plans. I wonder and I wish it had been different. It was really difficult not to get to say goodbye to the people who were such a big part of my life. They just disappeared all at the same time—it felt like a death of so many. And also the death of me as I had known myself to be. Tragedy on multiple levels.

———————

I don't remember leaving the country. I don't remember driving across the border. I don't remember if our car was searched that time and what time of day it was when we left. I don't remember looking at my room or our apartment for the last time thinking, *Goodbye forever.* But I do remember knowing that I wasn't sure I would be allowed to come back; thinking this over and over as I held on tightly to my favorite teddy bear Kajtek. Although we were being sponsored to come to the USA by an organization called the

International Rescue Committee and arriving as legal political refugees, we were leaving Poland illegally. Escaping. Fleeing. Running for our lives. This was what seeking freedom looked like.

# CHAPTER 3

# Stuck in Purgatory

## Bad Soden, Germany
## 1987

Our first stop on the journey to freedom was a refugee camp in Germany. It was in a town named Bad Soden and the facilities were located next to a big forest. There were lots of tall, green trees behind the buildings and a small town with regular life going on in the other direction. The residents of Bad Soden went about their business going to the grocery store, the pharmacy, and running daily errands. We were the only ones in purgatory, waiting for our new life to begin.

We were supposed to remain there for a couple of weeks as our arrangements in the United States were being finalized. We lived in what looked like a two-star European hotel where I slept on a pull-out sofa with my sister in the living room. This was okay since Ania and I always shared a room and she sometimes ended up next to me when she was scared at night. We also shared a bed when we traveled to Greece in our camper, and really, anytime we were on vacation I'd end up with her on a single bed. We had a trick to make more space for each other: sleeping in the opposite direction from one another, like upside down. She'd put her pillow where my feet were and I'd do the same. This really only worked when we were little because as we got taller, we really didn't want to wake up to each other's feet greeting us in the mornings. So by the time we were sharing the sofa in Bad Soden, we just slept alongside each other. It was strange, though, to fold out a couch and have that be my place for the night, not having my own bed or my own space, just a corner in the living room.

There wasn't much space for all four of us, and we had to share one small bathroom. My parents were in the one bedroom and Mores somewhere in between that room and the living room.

The very best thing about Bad Soden was being reunited with our dog. We drove about four hours to pick him up, my parents' friends meeting us in Hanover to make the drop-off. We pulled up to their car, the trunk opened, and our Mores jumped out onto the ground. He was traveling with the blanket he slept on, which was on my bed before we got him and my blanket became his blanket. I cried when I saw him. It was a reminder of home and he was a lost family member back with us again.

I'd wake up in the middle of the night sometimes and cry into his welcoming and understanding fur. No words were needed. Just a warm presence and a sense of being held. But it was all fine. It was just a bit lonely and unsettling, especially since we didn't speak but a few words of German.

Outside of the building with the rooms where we slept and "lived" was another structure. It contained the kitchen and restaurant facilities just down a few steps. It was more like a cafeteria. We ate all our meals there with all the other people, also awaiting their turn to fly to the place with a better future. Poor Mores had to be tied to a railing outside the cafeteria building and we ate close to a window so we could see him. It made me uncomfortable.

We met other Polish families and the adults shared advice and information about the process. I think there may have been a girl or two close to my age, but it just felt like the parents were all really pressuring us all to bond so that we would not be so lonely and scared. Maybe if we looked like we were having fun playing together, they would feel less doubt and discomfort about what was happening (or not happening as we waited). I didn't want to make friends. I understood this to be temporary, so why make friends whom you'd have to leave quite soon?

While we waited, we had a few English lessons and a couple workshops on life in America. These were mainly for the adults and I attended out of boredom, but also because I felt more like a grown-up than a kid really. There was nothing to do and the town was very small, but we heard from the others that the average wait time was about fourteen days. I counted down as we watched others go.

Ironically, the worst thing that happened in Bad Soden was being reunited with Mores. Someone realized that the dog was not included in the original immigration paperwork. Chicago was initially our destination. This now had to change because the place that was ready for us to move into apparently did not accept refugee dogs, humans only. The two weeks in Germany turned into several months as summer came and went. Fall started, the weather became chilly, and leaves turned from green to yellow and brown and fell from trees. I watched the local kids with their shiny new backpacks start a new school year and I was so envious. I thought about my friends back in Szczecin starting seventh grade. I wondered if they were waiting for me to come back from Italy and then later, after not seeing me, wondering what happened. I imagined my teacher calling out attendance and nobody knowing why I was absent. I missed them all. I even missed the classes I hated (mainly that was gym).

Our stay in the temporary refugee camp started looking a bit less temporary when my sister, who befriended a little girl who lived in the town somehow, started to attend school with her. I guess she went because there was nothing else to do and it gave her a way to be involved in something and not to sit in the confusion of what the heck was actually happening with our life. So I watched her, too, put on a backpack and go to classes, smiling at a little girl leading her through the process. It made me so much more sad and lonely. So confused.

A large part of me wondered if all this was just not going to work out, if we could return and go back to our old life, our old house, our old room. I actually hoped and prayed that would happen. I longed to see my family, my friends, and my classmates. I cried at night for my bed, my room, my home, my school, my city, my country. I missed everyone and everything. I missed being around people who knew me. I didn't understand what was happening, only that there was this overwhelming sadness inside and I didn't know what to do with it. It was heartbreaking.

I welcomed my thirteenth birthday like this, that September. Not with friends, cake, laughter, presents, balloons, and games. Alone. Isolated. With sadness and fear as my companions. I was transitioning from a child to a teenager, but facing very adult experiences at the same time. It meant having to grow up faster than I was ready for, than anyone should have to.

"You look so good, honey. You've lost weight!" my mom said to me that day.

I was wearing jeans and my favorite black-and-blue-checkered flannel shirt. My hair was tied back into a ponytail and I was outside playing Chinese jump rope, a game with elastic rope made of rubber bands involving jumping and chanting. Normally I'd play it with my friends, but my dad and my sister were filling in that day, and for a while at that time. Despite playing, I felt anything but good. I wanted words to help me make sense of my internal state, despite of how I may have looked on the outside. But they were not there—just the turmoil within me. Somehow I assumed that my pain, everything I felt, wasn't meant to be visible or talked about. This made me withdraw deeper in and feel even more alone.

Nonetheless, I smiled and said "Thank you."

It was a time of living in between worlds (out of Poland and not yet in America) and forever waiting on the unknown—my young girl's life put on hold while I held my breath unsure of what I was anticipating, not knowing what was coming. Hoping for something incredible but fearing the worst. I wondered if perhaps we could stay and somehow start over in Germany instead. It was only across the border from Poland, a few hours' drive. Much of it was familiar already because we had visited and traveled through it many times. I liked it there and I loved West Berlin. It felt like a fancy big city. It seemed so much safer to be a short distance from family and the old well-known places. It was comforting to think that I could see my grandpa much more easily. America just seemed so foreign and so far. It was frightening sometimes.

Finally in mid-November, it was our turn to go. Our paperwork was approved and we were given a new destination—New York City—apparently international dogs were allowed in the Big Apple. I wondered if American barking translated easily into Polish barking. We made jokes about Mores making new doggie friends in the USA.

---

We flew on TWA. I slept with my head on my mom's lap, covered with the rough, thin airline blanket. Back in those days there was still a smoking section on transatlantic flights, and I never really understood how that was supposed to work. Was there an invisible wall keeping the secondhand smoke out of the nonsmoking seats? I had only been on an airplane once before, one way to Paris, with my mom when I was about four. No cigarettes there. Being on planes wasn't a thing people like us did often back then, if at all. Not in Poland, anyway, and not even when the neighboring kids thought you were "rich." As the huge airline jet hit the landing strip in the land of the free, everyone on the flight erupted in cheering and clapping. A mixture of fear and excitement rushed through my body.

We arrived at John F. Kennedy Airport in New York City at the old TWA terminal. Our dog traveled in cargo in a special cage Papuś had built for him from plastic milk crates he gathered at grocery stores in Germany. It was green. He made a small wooden panel and screwed it securely to the top where my sister and I painted our dog's name with hearts and flowers. "My name is Mores," it said, in English. Arriving at JFK, one of the world's busiest airports, when you are thirteen and don't speak the language is overwhelming, to say the least. (Hell, arriving there as an American adult is overwhelming!) I don't have recollection of most of it—how we got off the flight, the immigration or customs process, getting our bags. I was in a state of shock. Then I heard our dog howling somewhere in the distance at the busy airport. That I remember vividly. His crate had apparently been delivered off the plane to baggage claim and we ran toward the noise to try to free him. The sounds he was making were terrible. I thought he was hurt or dying. There was a lot of drama and confusion, and we could not get him released. For what seemed like eternity, my parents tried to communicate with customs officers in charge of the poor pup. Some paperwork or permits were missing—we didn't understand exactly. The whole time I sobbed, my body shaking, my heart aching seeing my dog, my best friend, suffering. He was howling and barking and clawing at the crate in an attempt to get out. It was horrible. I am not sure how my parents navigated the process, not knowing the language, but I think someone finally took pity on the two distraught young girls crying for their doggie. We got our bags and our Mores and headed outside the terminal. The flight had been long. We were jetlagged, emotionally exhausted, stressed, and scared. We looked for and waited for our ride, which was supposed to meet us, but nobody came. *Nobody came!* We waited an hour. Two hours. Three and then four. We had a phone number to contact and some US dollar bills but no one told us that in order to use a pay phone (back when those were a regular thing to use and cell phones were not yet around) you had to dial a 1 before the area code. My dad kept trying over and over with no luck. I even had a shot at it. We just kept hearing a recording we didn't understand on the other end of the line. It was hours and hours and to me it seemed like eternity. Between my body's exhaustion and devastating tears, I was sure all this was just a bad idea. I wanted it to be a nightmare I'd eventually wake up from, but no such luck. We must have had help getting quarters and finally dialing correctly and reaching someone because a man came. He came in an ugly, long minivan and spoke fast and foreign words.

We were taken to our temporary housing, which was in Flatbush. It was an old apartment shared with other new arrivals. Everyone shared one bathroom and it was filthy, stinky, smelly, and crawling with roaches. I'm not sure how and what we slept on, but I do remember the one bathtub being so dirty, my mom said not to sit in it but bathe standing up. We poured warm water over our bodies using a small cooking pot. It was awful, disgusting, and so extremely shocking I only have one memory from the time there. It was the first time we got out to go for a walk, to find something to eat, our first experience in America on our own. It was night. It was dark. My dad held the dog close to us on his leash. He was sniffing around the sidewalks getting to know the new surroundings. We all needed food and I wanted a fancy fizzy drink—a red Coca Cola or maybe the green Sprite—the kind we only could get in Germany and not in any of the stores in Poland. We walked to a small local grocery store, bought a few things, and were ripped off by the cashier who short-changed us. Once we realized this, we had no language skills to go back and fight for the money he actually owed us. This was how we arrived in the United States. While the days of my childhood in Poland were filled with grayness and fear, the next phase of my life was colored in black and pure shock. It was not what I had hoped for. It was not what I was promised. It was not at all what I had prepared for. This was not "freedom."

Eventually a permanent apartment was found for our family as well as jobs for my parents and schools for Ania and me. Before Christmas that year, we moved into a two-bedroom apartment on the fourth floor of 21 Cropsey Avenue in Brooklyn, New York.

Little did I know that the worst part of my life was just beginning.

# CHAPTER 4

# Land of the Free

In the fall of 1987, we found ourselves in New York City, in a small old Bensonhurst apartment in the borough of Brooklyn, the four of us and Mores. We arrived there with $1,200 of life savings (and a loan from the International Rescue Committee for the airline tickets, which probably exceeded that amount), several suitcases of clothes and belongings, and, as they say, the shirts on our backs. The most important piece of baggage was a brown leather bag shaped like an old-fashioned doctor's bag, back when they made house visits. It contained all of our documents and legal paperwork as well as the selected few old family photos we were able to bring with us. Of course, the gigantic green, plastic home-made "dog crate" that became Mores's new dog house came with us too. My dad figured out a way to disassemble it and put it back together so it was easier to transport it. None of us spoke much English.

The apartment was dark and had a strange, dusty, old smell to it. To the left of the entrance was a small bathroom and a long hallway, which wrapped around the kitchen and led to the living room and my parents' bedroom. Across the kitchen, to the right off the long hallway, was the bedroom I shared with Ania. It had a maroon carpet and dark-brown floor-to-ceiling fake wooden panels on the walls. The ceiling was white and looked like someone did a sloppy paint job on it, strange textured painting that looked like it was dripping down. The windows had metal safety bars in them, even though they only opened halfway, which made it feel like jail (not exactly an image of the "freedom" I was hoping for). The view out the window was of the back side of a small park, jogging track, and basketball courts. We would later call it the "drug dealers" park and avoid it after dark when walking our dog or coming home from school.

We bought mattresses to sleep on in Coney Island with the help of the man who was so late to pick us up at JFK. I never forgave him for leaving us helpless and stranded for so long at the airport even though he bought us hot dogs, which we tasted for the first time that day. We tied the mattresses to the roof of his ugly station wagon, which had brown wooden panels on the sides. The mattresses were also really ugly, brown and orange flowers on a cream-colored background with a brown base. This new setup felt kind of like camping, sleeping on a mattress. Except that you put this one on a wooden box (covered in the same old-lady floral-patterned fabric) and then you put it on metal rods with legs or wheels. In America they called this a bed.

Our first trips to the grocery store were stressful, but we learned a lot at Waldbaum's in those early days. For example, the fact that there was no "real" bread, just this square, spongy "toast bread" stuffed into plastic bags and cut up into slices. It looked nothing like the hard, round loaves we were used to. Obviously, you just used it for the toaster. Cheese here was very strange. Cottage cheese did not resemble any cheese we had ever seen before and American cheese was orange, plastic, sliced, and wrapped in clear individual pockets. It kind of looked like wax. It kind of tasted like it might have been wax too. Milk in America came in huge plastic jugs with handles or in cardboard cartons, not glass bottles, and you could not find just regular milk—it was all either vitamin D or low fat or skim—which was confusing. Apparently, everyone here ate a cold breakfast called "cereal," which you covered with cold milk in a bowl, and not just Corn Flakes (which we had seen, tasted, and mispronounced in Europe before). There was a whole aisle dedicated to the stuff and it came in all sorts of colors and shapes! Almost nobody drank hot tea at least three times a day like we did with breakfast, dinner, and supper, sometimes also at afternoon tea time. We were introduced to a new meal called "lunch" and discovered that people didn't really have suppers in New York. The grocery stores were filled with an abundance of foods and everything came in several options, brands, and varieties. It was impossible to decide which one to buy, so we just bought the least expensive versions. Also, everything was very big or came in large quantity packs 6, 12, 24, jumbo, giant, family size, XXXL! It was overwhelming.

We discovered that American supermarkets (unlike those in Germany where we had just come from) were not dog friendly. For months, we talked about how the four of us were strolling around a grocery store with Mores on a leash one day. We laughed about him shopping for meat in the deli section. Apparently, we were being paged over the loudspeaker to please remove the dog from the store but understood none of it. Eventually someone escorted us out with the poor (but well-behaved) animal. I was so embarrassed and ashamed. This is how the first few weeks and months looked, figuring things out and learning by making mistakes. Trial and error—but mostly error, it felt like—screwing up all the time. *Ugh.* These were some very difficult lessons, and I took it all so hard.

We bought a hexagon-shaped table with a glass top and four chairs with wicker backs at a store "not too far away." We carried them home on our backs for several blocks. It required a few trips back and forth because there were so many boxes and they were heavy. We didn't have a car. It was almost winter and it was a cold and dark afternoon, but the enthusiasm carried us through it. The last trip for the final boxes I made with my dad alone. I considered myself the strong one, always the helper. Eventually we purchased a used car and went to Ikea for the basics and started to make a home in our new apartment. And along with us, so did the roaches—but I guess technically, they were there first. I would often walk into the kitchen in the middle of the night to get a glass of water and see them scurrying away, escaping the light, on tops of the counters. I'd stomp my feet real loud walking in, waiting to open my eyes just a few seconds longer than needed, hoping to scare them so I would not have to see them. It was disgusting. What was also disgusting was the floor in the kitchen. It was made from fake tiles that resembled rubber and felt super sticky with grease right around the stove, so sticky that our slippers would stick to it when we walked in there. And it wasn't our grease but someone else's who had lived there before. Yuck.

We arrived in mid-November and at some point, shortly after, I went to a local junior high school, where the culture shock was indescribable. No workshop on America in the German refugee camp prepared me in any small degree for what I faced and had to deal with, process, and reconcile by myself at thirteen. In Poland, we wore uniforms to school (dark blue with the school emblem sewn on our sleeves and white collars) and sat in silence (with a proper straight-up posture) while the teacher lectured. We had to raise our hands in order to be given permission to speak. We sat in desks of two with our school bags by our feet and our notebooks and fountain pens neatly placed in front of us. We had lots of homework, studying, reading, reciting things in front of the class the next day as well as written and oral exams, like being interrogated about the chapters we had to read the night before, in front of an audience of your peers. It was a stressful, rigorous, and extremely controlled process. Lots of rules and regulations. I learned to follow them well. I was a serious student. I worked hard and was one of the top students in my class. It was competitive and intense but I had the system down. And this was just elementary school!

I was placed in seventh grade at a public school in Brooklyn, which was a good twenty-minute walk from our new home. What I remember from there isn't much, as I was in a state of complete and utter shock. All of it is just stored in my mind as this one frozen scene in time—walking into the classroom. I couldn't tell you what subject it was. First of all, I was bewildered at the fact that kids could chew gum in class and talk to each other inside the classroom (that was only allowed in the hallways back home during breaks in between classes). Walking into the classroom before the bell rang was like walking into utter chaos—people everywhere, sitting on top of desks, yelling, laughing, screaming, running around—it was a zoo. I was used to sitting in the classroom in silence whether the teacher was in there or not. You whispered with your friends before class started. I could not believe the clothes these kids wore, how extremely loud they were, and how some boys sat with their feet on top of their desks—with shoes on! They threw paper balls across the room, and all the desks were single-person and completely disorganized all over the room, not in straight rows or lines. The teacher was having a hard time getting control over the kids and all the noise so he yelled louder over the students. Then he whistled. I was stunned.

Because I was a foreigner, I was assigned a helper who was supposed to (I can only assume) assist me in adapting to the new school. I did not speak English besides a couple of basic sentences about what my name and age were and asking "How do you do?" (which nobody said anymore, at least not in Brooklyn). Because I was Polish, I was put together with a Russian-American girl and that somehow made sense to everyone but me. I am guessing they thought we could communicate easily because the countries were close together on a map?! I did take a couple of years of Russian in school in Szczecin (my helper did not speak Polish) because it was required in the Communist times. I did not, however, know enough to navigate the challenges of junior high school in conversation. The girl who got picked for this job was not pleased about it and rolled her eyes a lot and giggled with her friends. I understood pretty quickly they were making fun of me—that language is international. So, while learning how to bake things in something called "Home Economics," I stepped out to go to the bathroom. Crazy thing, you did not need permission, you just left the class and went! I locked myself in the bathroom stall and cried. My helper certainly appreciated the break from having to babysit me. This was the only other memory from the Brooklyn Junior High experiment. This one wasn't of shock but raw pain instead.

In the afternoons as I walked home alone, I was frequently followed, ridiculed, and bullied. Eventually I was beaten up as well, always by girls in my school. I learned that in English (in Brooklyn) you called this "getting jumped"—it happened regularly in that neighborhood—and hoped that if I called it by the American name, it wouldn't hurt so much. The girls learned pretty quickly that I did not fight back or run or cry so they would surround me in a circle and kick and push me and pull my hair while yelling things at me that I didn't understand. I stood there proudly not giving in, holding my head up high—I was strong and brave—I was not going to let them get to me. Somehow, I didn't really feel the physical pain much. I felt frozen on the outside. Inside, though, everything hurt like hell.

My parents were at work so by the time I made it home from school early in the afternoon, the house was empty, except for the dog. Once the bullies had enough and left me at my front door, I went inside, crawled into bed, curled myself in a ball, and sobbed. I cried so hard my breath failed me sometimes and my heart raced, pounded, and ached all at the same time. After a while I settled myself down and rolled onto my back (Mores my only friend and witness) and stared at that weird-looking white ceiling, in my ugly brown room, lying on my strange mattress that was supposed to be my bed.

"Why?!"

I asked this question a lot of myself ... and maybe of God.

"Why???!!!"

Eventually, after a week or a month, I couldn't tell you, I refused to go back. I was inconsolable, heart-broken, and felt utterly and completely alone. All I wanted was to go back home. Real home. *My* home.

Christmas came and the constant feelings of intense sorrow, loss, and grief only got worse. The holidays were always such an amazing affair back home. We had a large family and lots of friends, and there were always parties, dinners with family, and festivities that seemed to go on forever. We attended a big cathedral for Christmas Mass too. I loved dressing up, being with my family, singing in church, preparing the table and meals for our guests. I loved when friends and family came over and when we got to go visit them. It was just such a celebration. The tree decorated with all the ornaments—same ones each December—the familiar, the traditional, the handed-down trinkets and sentimental pieces. We would spend time together each year making chains out of colorful construction paper and then adding them to the tree. All the little details, the elegant clothes, the fancy tablecloths, and the good plates and silverware. The same familiar smells, tastes, and sounds of the holidays. It was magical every year!

The first American Christmas, it was just the four of us. We had no one. We had nothing. Everything that reminded me who I was and where my place in the world was had vanished. I had no point of reference. I had no proper farewell, no grieving process, so neither did I have any closure. Nothing made sense. It was a complete loss of identity and orientation at the age of thirteen. I could not fully understand how that would affect me as a person and a woman until much later in life. That December, all I ached for and desperately wished for was to go back to the life we left behind.

With the New Year came a new school for me: St. Finbar Elementary. It was a small Catholic school within walking distance from home, thankfully in the other direction from my first one. This school had uniforms and a bit more structure and discipline, which I welcomed with relief. The class sizes were smaller, and the teachers were pleasant and more involved with the kids (and slightly more in control of the class environment as well). The kind principal was an older Italian gentleman who reminded me of Santa Claus. His hair was gray, and he had a long white beard and a big round belly. He was warm, listened, and seemed heartbroken when he heard the story of my first days in the American school system. He checked in on me regularly. We couldn't afford tuition at this private school, but he allowed me to attend for a minimal fee. I felt supported by the adults at the school. I especially loved my math teacher, Mrs. Russo. She had short, curly blonde hair, long pink fingernails, and a huge inviting smile. She quickly learned that I was a whiz in math. In reality, math had been my worst subject up till that point. My dad had to tutor me back in Poland. But we were just further ahead in terms of the subject matter covered and so I was now advanced—in math!!—a first!! I loved it. Especially when I got called up to the blackboard to solve problems for the rest of the class. I couldn't speak English, but I could speak numbers (even though some of them looked a little different when I wrote them). It felt so good to be recognized and praised for something. It felt so refreshing to be getting something right, rather than wrong all the time. It was extremely encouraging and so much needed. Pretty soon the kids were cheating off my paper on exams. Silly them, they also did this on vocabulary quizzes in English class, which was (obviously!!!) a terrible idea. Mrs. Russo also taught us vocab and, because she was a saint, always gave me an 80 percent, no matter how badly I did. My poor cheating neighbors did not have the same luck (nor the grades).

The work was difficult, intense, and, at times, impossible. My English was still minimal so I had to do all my homework and reading with a dictionary. No Google nor Google Translate at the time. Getting any assignment done meant translating every word just to understand what was being asked of me, then translating the actual assignment or reading or questions. Next I had to write out my answer in Polish (since I did all my thinking in my native language) and later translate what I had composed into English using the dictionary once more. It took all afternoon and sometimes lasted well into the night. Some days, I just wouldn't be able to finish and fell asleep on top of my books. There were a lot of tears and frustration. Most of the teachers were very understanding and accommodating. But then there was Sister Hyacinth.

In her royal-blue habit and round black glasses, rather round herself, pink-faced and extremely unpleasant, Sister Hyacinth terrified me. I think everyone was afraid of her. Sister Hyacinth taught us religion. I understood almost nothing.

Sister Hyacinth decided it would be a good idea to make me read the Bible out loud to the others in class. I am not sure why she did this, besides some obviously un-Christian pleasure she might have gotten out of the experiment. I could not pronounce the majority of the words. I did not know what I was reading or mispronouncing. She loved correcting me. She would yell at me and her cheeks would get super rosy and then her whole face would turn red. She called me an idiot. She screamed and yelled and waved her finger. She used my "favorite" method of clarifying things—speaking s-l-o-w-e-r and LOUDER—as if I was not foreign but just really, really dumb. And hard of hearing. I sat there drowning in embarrassment and shame. I was in the first row, right in front of her desk. I think I cried once right there, in my single-person desk, books neatly tucked into the space under the seat, my glasses fogging up from the tears, my head sinking low, and my shoulders slumping forward. Fuck, this was hell.

For a very long time after these incidents, well after the school year ended, Sister Hyacinth showed up regularly in my nightmares. She usually held a ruler and would slap it on my desk or the teacher's table. I'm not sure if this actually happened in real life or if it was a little colorful detail my imagination added while I slept. Either way, religion was not my favorite subject. Hopefully God had a little chat with Sister Hyacinth when she got to heaven at the end of her life and He cleared this up for me. Maybe He got some angels together and they all "jumped her"—Brooklyn style—when she was the new kid in the neighborhood up there. Sadly, I did not learn love in religion class. I learned more fear.

Despite Miss Russo and the wonderful principal, embarrassment and shame were my constant companions in eighth grade. We got so close and used to each other that they stuck around for a very, very long time. I stumbled and misstepped my way through those six months of school and eventually made a few friends. I had my first crush on a boy. I got invited to my first sleepover. I attended my first school dance. My mom made my dress with a matching bow for my hair—they were both black and white with polka dots—and we bought shiny black shoes from Payless. I danced to Madonna's "Material Girl" with the Santa Claus principal, but also with the kids! I participated in something called "graduation" wearing a golden yellow cap and gown. I didn't understand why we had to dress up in these weird costumes made of polyester. Especially in the summer, when graduation took place. The ugly, large mustard-yellow robe covered up my pretty dress and made me sweat. The hat was the worst thing about the outfit with a tight rubber band running across my forehead to keep it on my head. There were endless rehearsals of weird walking to strange music and a ceremonial moving of the strings that hang from the top of the hat, to the other side of your face. It was called a tassel and it symbolized the fact that we were leaving elementary school and had earned our diplomas. I certainly didn't earn mine. I just got here. "From a Distance" by Bette Midler was our class song. I still have a hard time not turning it off when I hear it now—it immediately induces the challenging feelings I was experiencing at that time.

Little by little I started to walk home from school with a couple of girls, mainly listening, just learning how to speak again. Once I started understanding what was being talked about, which always comes first before you start speaking a foreign language, I had moments where I wondered if I was better off not knowing and just nodding and smiling like a moron instead. Because it is such a strange and suffocating feeling when you have something you want to say and just don't have the words to do it yet. They come slow, not conjugated right, mispronounced ... often they don't come at all. Thus, the thought sits there inside of you brewing, boiling, and growing desperate to be shared. You can sense how it makes you feel, you know what you would like to be able to say, you see others talking about it, but you cannot express your own experience. You cannot contribute or participate. It is almost like being silenced by an overwhelming force—being muzzled—having no voice of your own among your peers. It is extremely disempowering: I felt helpless and was often overtaken by pure despair. Embarrassment moved in, too, and anger. Then the moment passed. I had, once again, missed the space where I could have added my part and connected with those around me. Shame washed over me. Isolation. Disconnection. Those familiar old friends. Then came resignation. *This is just how it is. This shitty experience? This is my fucking life. There is nothing I can do to change it. And maybe nobody actually cares about what I have to say anyway. I'm stupid.* The world went on without me adding my two cents. I was left feeling kind of there, but also sort of transparent, nobody seeing or caring about me. Life was happening around me, but without me in it. I took up space and smiled and sort of looked like everyone else—but inside I was dying because my heart was constantly breaking and I couldn't use my voice and express myself, tell others who I was.

It was a kind of prison—me alone looking out at the world around me from within a cell, which was my own self. I felt stranded and stuck inside my own body—like it was a cage separating me from a real-life experience. It was surreal.

When you experience this, you look like you are with people, but truly, you are so very alone, in your jail cell, withdrawn within, to the very back corner, the darkest spot. You sit in your cage and you observe the others, who are usually enjoying themselves. You know you'll never get out nor will anyone come to rescue you because you're the alien. (They actually call you "resident alien" when you first arrive, but really *alien* is just as appropriate because it's what they really mean: "someone from another planet.") Your words are foreign. And so is your experience. No one can help you because they actually don't even see you. You suffer alone, on the inside, while walking home from school and everyone talking all around you and laughing. It is excruciating.

I very often wondered, *What is wrong with me? Why am I not like them?* And people had no way of knowing the pain I was carrying inside, so I was just labeled the "weird, shy, quiet, dumb one." But that wasn't me at all. I wasn't any of those things. But the verdict was reached, and it seemed like no one cared about the truth. They just moved on to the next thing. I felt invisible and worthless.

I withdrew into those inner conversations (self-judgment, self-criticism, victimhood) and came to the conclusion that there was just something not right with me, something at my very core.

I was not like the others. I could never be like them. I did not belong. Because I was broken. I was so convinced of this, of being all alone and not enough, that I never brought it up with the people I could talk to—my parents and sister. I was too ashamed to even discuss it. I remained isolated, suffered in silence, and cried myself to sleep at night.

---

My parents both received jobs in Manhattan. They got up early in the mornings and took the train, which was called the subway or the metro in New York City. They began their American careers by working together in an antique shop. My mom was a cleaning lady who dusted old furniture. My dad worked in the stock room during the day and took on a night shift as a doorman somewhere. (I'm not sure when he slept.) Their boss was especially belittling and mean. It is amazing how many people we encountered early on who were just incredibly cruel to us rather than compassionate, empathetic, and helpful. I never understood that. I remember one thing they kept repeating to us in the refugee camp in Germany because it gave me so much hope. "Almost nobody in America is *from* America. We all come from somewhere else. It is the great melting pot of cultures and people." It sounded so wonderful. However, that was not my experience in those early days. Most people were all too eager to forget when, how, and from where they arrived in the Land of the Free. They did not relate to my struggles. Instead, they chose to use me as a target of their own frustrations, power plays, and amusement. It felt cruel and almost sadistic and again, so very isolating. My parents had the same experience in their first job. It was crushing especially for my mom who was a beloved celebrity in Poland before the life of sweeping dust off old junk in America. It was like who we all were before was irrelevant and erased. Nobody gave a shit about any of it.

*Is this freedom?* I wondered. *It doesn't feel very good.*

My sister, Ania, landed in a school called St. Michael's and from the beginning made friends and had kind teachers. I guess because she was almost three years younger, it was just a little bit easier for her. She was dealing with kids, whereas I was dealing with teenagers. Kids were more accepting of our foreignness. They could see things that teenagers and adults forgot how to see—that we just wanted to belong and to play. I'm not saying it was easy for her, just maybe a little less terrible. She still missed home, too, I know. It was hard on us all.

We cycled through states of shock, denial, misery, alienation, longing, and confusion. We also took turns crying and wondering whether coming to America was a mistake, or perhaps we took turns *knowing* it was a mistake. It was paralyzing. I felt a deep sense of desperation to undo all this, especially while watching my parents suffer. Their despair often weighed on me so heavily and was extremely destabilizing. In the midst of my own loneliness, seeing them struggle meant I had no one to go to for comfort and support. This was a conclusion I came to myself. I couldn't possibly add to their worries and heartache. I needed to alleviate pain from them by sorting things out for myself. So they had one less thing to be upset about: my fucked-up situation and my feelings about it.

So I stuffed my own pain deeper within, was "brave and responsible," and distracted myself by working harder at surviving. I had to grow up quickly and figure out quite a bit of the new stuff on my own. My parents could not help me with homework—they did not speak the language. They could not help me navigate the social challenges school presented—they did not understand the culture. They could not help me with the teachers because of both those things. In reality, this slowly gave birth to a new tension between us, a tension that I imagine exists within most immigrant families. My parents' lack of understanding of American culture and viewing everything through the lens of our Polish culture left me stuck trying to be one way for their sake and being another way for the acceptance of my peers. It was a very delicate balance, keeping some of the old culture while adjusting to and taking on the new. I feared letting go of the only way I knew to be (also the only way of being me my parents knew), and I feared becoming the new way because I didn't yet understand it (and because my parents might not accept or like me that way). It felt like two massive forces were violently pulling at me from opposite directions. While my parents would often remind me how lucky I was because I got to pick the best of both cultures and keep what I liked, I often felt they meant that they would get to choose for me. When my actions were "too American," I would certainly hear about not maintaining tradition or forgetting my roots. It was an impossible thing to navigate. Especially as a teenager. I dealt with it by sharing less and less with my family—hiding parts of myself more and more—because I felt that I wasn't heard or understood. It took so much energy to explain something challenging I had gone through at school and then have to educate my parents about why it mattered or why it happened because in Poland it just wasn't like that. They simply had no point of reference, no understanding. So the child in me who came to her parents for comfort and advice ended up of explaining or teaching. It was exhausting and confusing. The conversation would always veer into, "What does that mean?" and lead to a million questions I would then have to answer. I never seemed to get the support I needed. I cried inside of my tiny closet or at night in my bed, found comfort in food, stared at that ugly white ceiling in my room, or lost myself in music or letter-writing to friends and family back home. In fact, I lived for letters arriving from abroad in our tiny mailbox. I checked the mail daily; the blue "AIR MAIL" sticker on an envelope never failed to put a smile on my face when I got home from school. Reading news from old friends took me away from the present-day reality. It was a much welcomed escape.

In order to help my parents and contribute to the family (as was expected) I took on a lot of responsibilities. I helped to cook. I cleaned. I walked the dog. I went to the grocery store. I watched over my sister. All while being in school full-time, which was more than a full-time job in itself given all the translating required. It was hard work and a hard life, especially for a child, which I still was. This is another dynamic so common in immigrating families, which leads to identity confusion and a complete loss of childhood for the refugee kids. Because we arrive with so little in terms of money, our parents go straight to work. They work hard jobs, long shifts, sometimes several jobs, and they are stressed and exhausted. We are left to care for our siblings and be on house duty—we lose our parents and we lose time to actually be children. The carefree, explorative childhood opportunities are replaced with having to work hard from very early on in life. This can stick with us for the rest of our lives: constantly being productive, responsible, and living out of scarcity. We may not understand what is happening while young, but we can sense that as immigrants we are thought of as "less than." This gets into our very bones and leads to the need to over-function in order to prove our worth—to others, certainly, but most of all to ourselves.

That first summer in America I worked two jobs, besides watching "The Price Is Right" and "Days of Our Lives" with my sister. I worked behind the counter of a bakery owned by a Jewish Russian lady and I babysat. The Russian lady at the bakery let me bring home leftover bread and pastries to my family at the end of my shift. I quickly learned about black and white cookies, rye bread, challah, and all sorts of something called "bagels" as well as the fact that New Yorkers wanted their coffee immediately. Especially first thing in the morning. New York is a tough place to land when you are not fluent in English or American culture. I spoke neither language well (not at all, really). In New York nobody has time to teach you or show you—everyone is busy and in a rush. It was a lot for me to take in. It amazed me how rude the people were and the mean things they would actually say— aloud to a kid. It wasn't just that the vocabulary wasn't there—milk, coffee, cream, butter, cream cheese, sliced bread versus whole loaf—I learned that quickly. But then there was the vocabulary of "black coffee" and "light coffee" and "lightly toasted" bagel versus "well done." Besides the words, I had to learn the expressions and idioms too. And the fact that everyone was just so cranky before they had their morning cup o' joe. My parents never drank coffee so I didn't understand the addiction. The job was stressful and I didn't like it. I did not see myself having a future in the baking industry. I actually did not see myself in America, if I had anything to say about it. I missed home constantly.

The following autumn, ten months after we arrived in the United States, I started over for the third time by entering high school. St. Finbar's gave me about five months of being shielded by a small school with small class sizes. The school was only elementary, so once I did the strange graduation ceremony in eighth grade, it was high school time. The pain inside was still constant, like a gaping hole in my heart, but now settling down a bit and becoming less raw. I learned how to numb it and hide from it by keeping busy and not thinking about what we left behind. In some ways, I finally started to accept that there was no going back. This sometimes made it harder rather than easier because the reality of that truth was tougher to swallow than the hope that the daily suffering wasn't permanent. I was still constantly uncomfortable, like a fish out of water, second–guessing and questioning everything I said and did. It felt like I was playing a new game, but someone forgot to tell me what the rules were. Now added to the challenge of adapting to this new way and place was making a transition into a large new school—Bishop Kearney, an all-girls Catholic school.

I was a quick study. As immigrant kids, we become quite adaptable because we are not really given a choice. It's a "sink or swim" kind of thing. And so, again, I observed and imitated. That was my strategy back then, like a chameleon. I learned how to take the public bus during morning rush hour in Brooklyn using a school bus pass. I learned how to do high school in the USA: make a schedule, read a schedule, switch classrooms, use a locker with a combination lock, how to put loose-leaf paper in a three-ring binder and what #2 pencils were. I discovered the dread of eating lunch in a huge cafeteria not knowing anyone and, equally scary, getting changed in a girls' locker room for physical education class. I had just turned fourteen so not only was I navigating the new country, new culture, and a new school, I was now also trying very hard to navigate adolescence. That was a lot of navigating a lot of new things. I learned that in America teenage girls shave their underarms and legs, and by using my dad's razor, I proceeded to give myself a huge cut on my right shin (I still have that scar today). I hid the fact that I did this from my parents because it wasn't normal for women or girls to shave in Poland at that time. I noticed girls wearing bras and asked for one. I noticed acne on my face and asked girls at the school what they do about it (the answer was Oxy10—maybe you remember it if you lived through the phase of pimples in the '80s). I saw them using deodorant, perfume, painting their nails, and putting on lipstick. And then there was the hairspray—OMG the hairspray—the afternoons at the end of the school day in the bathroom of an all-girls Catholic high school were insane. I don't know how we did not die inhaling all those chemicals, but it definitely was hard to breathe. I really had to fight for a spot in front of the mirror in the ladies' room once classes ended for the day because the public bus that stopped right in front of our school was coming from the all-boys Catholic school St. Xavier's. So everyone needed hairspray and lipstick urgently at 2:30 p.m. All of these things happened in America much earlier in a young girl's life than where we came from. I had never kissed a boy. I had never been on a date. Right before I left Szczecin, the kids from school just started hanging out together socially, in groups. They just started using the home phone to call me and ask if I could join a few of them at the movies. We had just all cut class together for the first time ever on April Fool's Day and spent the time roaming around the area of the city by the shipyard. It was my first taste of fun and freedom with my peers and I had to leave it all behind. In America there were already boyfriends and girlfriends and competition among the girls to get *the* boy. (You won if you teased your hair just right, rolled up your skirt, and opened up a few buttons on your shirt, I discovered.) It was all so foreign to me. Mostly I learned how these things worked by comparing myself to other girls and noticing quite well and in a lot of detail where I was lacking. My hair wasn't right. My nose was too long. My glasses were too big. My breasts were too small. My body was too fat. I wasn't as pretty. I would never ever be like the rest of them. Always the outsider—this became my comfort zone—the only way I knew myself. The one that didn't fit in. The one who didn't belong. The foreigner.

My homeroom teacher freshman year of high school was Sister Barbara. Sister Barbara did not like me. (What was it with me and nuns?!) Sister Barbara had short curly brown hair, very bitten fingernails, and a freckled face. She also taught us social studies, which apparently was history. She was tall and slim and had a funny curve to her upper spine which gave her a crooked posture and a hunched back. She did not wear the typical nun's outfit as some of the other sisters but was very fond of a calf-length jean skirt that she wore almost daily. She did not smile very much. And she totally had it out for me.

I had to walk a good ten to fifteen minutes from home to the public bus stop each morning. When it was winter, I put what I called pantyhose on under my skirt. (Maybe you call them tights or leggings. I was always confused about that.) They were "nude" or "sheer" and I paid extra attention to be sure they came close to my skin color. The idea was to keep warm but for them to be unnoticed. I put socks over them and then my shoes. It was freezing in the winter with a skirt on! The public bus dropped me off right next to the school. It was about twenty-five blocks from start to finish and sometimes I would get delayed in rush-hour traffic. On those days, I had no time to run to the bathroom to remove the pantyhose, replace my knee socks and shoes, and be on time to class. Not being on time meant I had to go through the front entrance, stop at the office and get a late pass, which meant detention, which was unthinkable. So if I was late, I ran straight off the bus, shoved my jacket in my locker, and then ran again to my seat in Sister Barbara's homeroom. Each and every one of those days, she would do this one mean Sister Barbara thing. It was like a game she played. I sat in the row in front of her desk, but three chairs back. She would sit at her teacher's table, lean over to her right to see me behind the two other girls who sat in front of me, then look me in the face with a smirk, and then look down to check my legs.

"Marta, are you wearing tights again?"

"Yes."

I knew what was coming next.

"Tights are not part of the school uniform!" she would then announce to everyone. "Please go to the bathroom and remove them."

Besides the humiliation of getting up in front of the whole class and experiencing lots of eye rolls in my direction from my fellow students, this meant that I would sometimes miss announcements, morning prayer, or the pledge of allegiance. But I took the darn tights off in the bathroom as requested and then did the walk of shame back to the class, pantyhose rolled up into a ball in the palm of my hand, head hanging low, back into my seat. I did not know how the other girls did it with bare legs in 30- or 20-degree weather. (Maybe they were driven to school by their parents?) When I talked about it with my mom and dad, I was absolutely forbidden to leave the house with bare legs in the middle of winter! Did I want to end up with a cold or worse, the flu?! So I played this cruel game with Sister Barbara, who stepped up her part and started to give me detention rather than asking me to take off the stockings. Detention for basically trying to keep warm in the winter. Go figure.

None of my teachers could get my name right during attendance. I waited as they recited a list of girls with normal names in alphabetical order by last name, tense and anxious, waiting for them to get to mine—Kobylińska. There was always a long pause, sometimes awkward laughter or a giggle or a strange stressed exhale, with the stunned eyes to accompany it on the part of the professor taking attendance. Like the very sight of my family name was shocking or funny or some kind of a mistake. Impossible that such a name could be expected to be deciphered and then said aloud. Hearing them try to say it made my face and the back of my neck burn hot with shame.

*Do I correct them or do I just let them butcher it completely?* I asked myself.

It was a rhetorical question. I wouldn't have been able to get a sound out of my mouth. I was dreaming of disappearing into my seat or being sucked into the ground beneath me instead. Embarrassed.

For that matter, many couldn't get my first name right either. Marta was often made into Martha or Maria. I wanted with all my heart to be Anne-Marie, Melissa, or Jennifer, like the other girls.

Some teachers just skipped me (first and last name) altogether. Again, I felt that either everyone was staring at me because I was so foreign and strange *or* nobody saw me because I was invisible and unseen.

Something happens to you when the very name you are given cannot be spoken, gets constantly mispronounced, and causes such bizarre reactions in people. You start to feel like those reactions people are having to your name, an essential part of your identity, are mocking the very thing you believe yourself to be. I hated the conflicts my name brought me, and I even started to hate my name. Did I really have to fight for such a basic thing, being called by my proper, unedited, unchanged, un-Americanized first name?

Most of the time I would simply laugh it off, raise my hand, and wave it to let them know I was "present." I did not want to make my teachers uncomfortable. I also did not want extra attention from the teacher to fall on me and then feel everyone's eyes in the classroom on me as well. I just said "Here." But in reality nothing about it was funny. Deep down inside, I was swimming in my embarrassment and shame, always the same, familiar undertone to my life experience at the time. Different. Set apart. Not belonging. The (resident) alien.

In December of my freshman year in high school, Grandpa came to celebrate Christmas with us. I was so excited to get to see him after such a long time—it felt like it had been forever! My parents gave me $40 one day and permission to get off the bus before my stop to go shopping for Christmas presents for the family. This was a huge fortune to me. I had never held that much money in my hand before, which was all mine to spend. I had big plans to take the whole afternoon strolling around on 86th Street, picking things for my family, and then wrapping them myself and hiding the presents somewhere until it was time to place them under the tree. I was looking forward to this so much that I told everyone at school who would listen.

I kept the money in a little special wallet in the front pocket of my school bag. Throughout the day, I would just touch that spot on my backpack and a surge of excitement would shoot through my body.

I changed for gym, put my uniform and my school bag in my locker and went to suffer through PE, which I still hated. Who invented the stupid game of dodgeball?! It's authorized bullying, if you ask me. And I was always the target. When I came back to my locker, I found the money missing. I looked around at the girls who were changing back into school uniforms to see who possibly could have done it. My locker was locked. My wallet was there. It was just the cash that was taken. Who could possibly have been so cruel? Which one of them had pretended to be my friend and then stolen from me? The betrayal and the violation of trust I felt were sickening. I could not hold back the tears. My dreams of Christmas with my family and beloved Grandpa were instantly shattered and all kinds of raw emotions boiled up to the surface as my body folded in half and I began to sob.

*There it is again!* I thought. *Any time I feel like things might start being okay, something horrible happens! Why? Why me? Why again?!*

Not only was I heartbroken for one of my "friends" to have done this, not only was it a ruined Christmas, I was also deadly afraid of what my parents would say when I told them I lost the money—a lot of money—all the money!!! I would be in so much trouble. I could not believe it. The tears were certainly about more than just the cash. It was not the end of the world, it just felt like it. I felt like a fool again, to have told the girls that I had the cash and how excited I was to get something thoughtful for my family members. Knowing that someone had taken that away from me and was somewhere watching me cry and finding joy in it. This is what made it so sickening. That someone did this intentionally, betraying my trust, stealing from me, and that person was now celebrating while I was distraught. It proved yet again that people cannot be trusted and that I would never belong. No matter what I did, didn't do, wished for, someone would always somehow take advantage of me and make me feel as awful as I did at that moment. I was weeping for stupidly believing this time the story would have a different ending. A happy ending. What a fool!

I ended up at the principal's office, not sure if it was to report the crime or just because I could not get myself together to go to the next class. I just could not stop crying. In the waiting room of the principal's office, I had to try to put words together to tell my story to the vice principal. I could barely breathe. I was hyperventilating and shaking all over. Somehow, she was able to decipher my dilemma from what I was trying to communicate. And then, a Christmas miracle happened! I did not even have to go to the principal, which in itself was scary and only happened when you were in the biggest of big trouble. Right there, this kind woman, whose name I can't even recall, took out $40 from her purse, put it in a white letter envelope, and handed it to me. She put her hand on mine and held it for a moment, squeezing tightly. I stared down at her long painted fingernails and the wrinkles on her hands. I felt the warmth of her skin touching mine. She looked right into my face, into my tear-filled, swollen, red eyes, and said everything I needed to hear without opening her mouth. And then she added, "Merry Christmas." It was the kindest, warmest, most generous, and loving thing that happened to me since we arrived in America. From that day on, anytime I passed by her office, I looked in and tried to catch her attention, meet her gaze, and just smile and nod. We had a secret pact and understanding. I was forever indebted to her and eternally grateful. I finally felt like someone was on my team. She was an angel who saved my Christmas and contributed toward restoring my faith in humanity.

In an effort to fix all this not-belonging, at some point in my freshman or sophomore year, I stopped telling teachers and, more importantly, all the students, that I was an immigrant. Actually, I had used the term "political refugee" up until then, which normally was met with strange and questioning blank stares, which made me feel like shit inside. I did not have an advocate or an advisor helping me manage my language issue or helping me to assimilate so I decided I was just going to fake it. I was sick of explaining myself, meeting with teachers outside of class to fill them in, asking for exceptions, and apologizing that I did not understand. It was making excuses and asking for forgiveness for just being myself. It felt extremely humiliating. The school made no accommodations or effort to help me settle in, so by tenth grade I was taking British Literature along with everyone else. Two years into being in America, I was writing essays on Charlotte and Emily Brontë, reading *Jane Eyre* and *Wuthering Heights*, and preparing to take the SATs.

*If the others can do it, so can I,* I told myself. I told myself this a lot. and it eventually became my truth.

My second year in high school, however, I failed biology. It was the first time I had failed anything. My grandpa was visiting us with his wife, who was a doctor, and she was certain she could help me with my biology struggles. What she did not understand, while going over anatomy and the human digestive system, was that this was just a result of the predicament I had gotten myself into. It wasn't an aversion to bio. It wasn't that the material was impossible. It wasn't that I was somehow challenged or dumb and couldn't learn how the human body functioned. I just could not keep up with the translating necessary to maintain my cover. I would fall asleep at night on top of my books, encyclopedias, and the dictionary again, unable to complete all of my assignments. Out of exhaustion, desperation, and fear of what happens when one fails a subject in school in America, I came clean to my biology teacher. I told him my story. I confessed my sins, asked for his forgiveness, and hoped for a show of mercy with a large side of grace. With a lisp and a heavy Italian accent, he pushed his nerdy glasses up on his long nose with his finger, promptly failed me, and sent me to summer school.

Still, things were getting a little easier. I was finally able to understand most words and sentences and carry on a whole conversation without getting lost or speaking with a thick accent. I stopped having to pause to find that word I couldn't think of or to talk around in circles when I didn't actually know the word I was looking for. I stopped translating everything from Polish in my head into English, and the new language became more fluent and natural. I even found myself dreaming in English. Most of the time I was able to get away with not looking or sounding any different from my peers. As a teenager and a foreigner, this was all I wanted. Just to blend in, to fit in, to belong. Not to be different. Not to look different. Not to sound different. Not to stand out. Not to be the exception. Not to get attention because I needed extra help. Not to feel like everywhere I went, I showed up lacking something and then had to make up for it. I learned that if I worked hard enough, I could catch up my language skills. I learned that if I observed well enough, I could look just like the other girls. I learned that if I listened and imitated well enough, I could pass for an American teenager myself. And the times I did were so incredibly rewarding. Not to feel the "un-belonging," the "not fitting in," the "foreign" parts to me. Not to feel like there was something broken, not right, something missing, something defective about me. Just like any high school kid, I wanted to find my people and feel like I was a part of a group who liked me. And by junior year, this started to happen. I knew how to tease my bangs, perm and hairspray my hair, put on Maybelline mascara,

CoverGirl blush, and Kissing Koolers lip gloss while blasting the newest Janet Jackson single from my cassette player. I knew to wear two pairs of scrunched down socks, roll up my uniform skirt, and I even had a pair of white Keds sneakers, a cool acid-wash jean jacket (with all the buttons on it you could possibly add), and a silver Sony Walkman. I sang in the choir. I took part in the school play. I participated in the talent show and signed up for Driver's Ed after school and learned how to drive in the Brooklyn traffic. My best friend's name was Maddie, and we got part-time jobs together at a local McDonald's. We would get together on weekends to go to the mall, concerts, movies, and school dances. Once, after our junior prom, I even slept over at Maddie's house. My parents never got used to the fact that American kids would sleep at friends' houses, but I wrangled permission for this special occasion. Maddie lived in the projects, and we spent the evening dancing in a nightclub in Manhattan thanks to fake IDs. We loved to dance; Maddie was an amazing dancer. She could do Michael Jackson's moonwalk like it was nobody's business! We saved up enough money working at Mickey Dee's (as we called it) to get a taxi back to her house after clubbing. I lied to my parents about how late we got in that night because I didn't want to get into it, the explaining. So I started having the life of a regular teenager and even getting into trouble! After a New Kids on the Block concert, Maddie and I decided to hang out outside of the band's hotel in Manhattan, completely losing track of time. We got some pictures of them coming in or out of the building; it was the most exciting thing that had ever happened to us. We were in love after all with the lead singer, Jordan! We didn't have cell phones (most people didn't back then), so I called home on the pay phone a few times. I got home by taking the metro, and it was way past my curfew. The sun was starting to come up! Papús was so angry he didn't speak to me for several days.

Less than four years after arriving in the US, along with everyone else in eleventh grade, I took the SATs to get into college—in English—with nothing like special accommodations, extended time, or an ESL (English as a Second Language) option. I know now that it exists, but back then nobody told me (probably because I stopped admitting that I needed help). I simply took the same exam as native speakers who had been hearing and speaking English for seventeen years, compared to my three. It was stressful for us all, and maybe even a little bit extra for me. But I was finally happy! I even started my very first business and had my first taste of what it meant to be a self-made American entrepreneur. I launched a monthly membership-based fan club for Jordan from the New Kids. I called it Jordan's Posse. I sold a newsletter, which I wrote, typed, and photocopied at a local tobacco shop (this was way before the internet), and rare video clips I purchased and edited together on VHS tapes. I placed a small ad in a *Teen Bop* magazine and the cash and checks kept coming in! My parents eventually took me to Chase Manhattan Bank where I opened my very first savings account. I was a successful female business owner making my own money. Here was a taste of what was only possible in America! *Life*, I started to think, *isn't so bad after all.*

I was getting into a rhythm, adapting to my new surroundings, and navigating life was not such a struggle anymore. How things worked—from buses, to stores, to school, to shopping, to payphones, all the little things that make life go—started to become something I just knew how to do. I didn't have to figure it out anymore. No more mysteries to solve or puzzles to make fit. I could just know. And the same with people and how they acted—I now understood the unspoken language, the customs, the gestures, the tone, what to say and how to say it, what was expected, how interactions worked, and how to behave as a member of this new culture and society. It all started to happen naturally. My proudest moment and complete confirmation of my finally "getting" how it all worked was an incident at a local mall. We had gotten on a public bus together as a family, along with a couple and their baby who were friends of ours. We were going to Radio Shack to buy a TV. The mission was a success, and upon exiting the store after the purchase, a few kids tried to pick-pocket my parents and the couple. They held the door for the baby's stroller and there was just enough commotion for me to notice that as the "kind" strangers were helping us through the door with the TV, the stroller, the baby, and all the things were also trying to steal a couple of wallets.

"Look out!" I yelled at my mom and dad. "Watch your coat pocket!"

The group of teenagers then started cursing me out and yelling at all of us. I felt the nervous energy of fear, excitement, and courage rising in me over the dirty words and bad names they called us. I understood them now. Proudly and loudly, I cursed back. Just once. Just loud enough to stand up for us all. No standing silent and frozen and taking it like when the girls would beat me up in the first few months after arriving and starting school. This time, I spoke up. I fought back. I yelled. I defended us all. I felt powerful and brave. I had found my voice again.

My immense relief was short-lived however. Soon after this victory, in the summer between my junior and senior year in high school, my parents announced we were moving. So, yet again, the rug was pulled out from under my feet. Crushed to leave my friends and the familiarity it had taken so much effort to build, feeling like I was going to have to learn everything over once more, I decided life could absolutely not be trusted. I would have to always live anticipating bad things. I could never get comfortable, settle in, and trust my fortune, because something drastic and unsettling would inevitably happen. There would be chaos and danger all over again. I was devastated but resigned to the fact that this was simply how the world worked, in completely unfair ways.

# CHAPTER 5

# Movin' On Up

I entered Baldwin Senior High School as a senior, right before my seventeenth birthday. Once again, I was the new kid in a place where others had been together for a while. Once again, I was the foreigner beginning anew. The comfort, which I worked so hard on obtaining, was gone and instability, insecurity and doubt surrounded me. Starting over somewhere new was trauma all over again—that feeling of being ripped out of the familiar and thrown into a new place having to relearn how to do life. At least this time I spoke the language and had an idea of what high school was like. But I did not understand that Americans living in the projects in Brooklyn are not the same Americans as in the predominantly white, privileged suburbs of Nassau County, New York. My friends in Brooklyn were mostly African American. They lived in small, overcrowded apartment buildings that looked like they were falling down. They taught me how to dress, how to dance, how to speak, and how to curse properly in English. In Baldwin, kids lived in big houses with long driveways and perfectly cut lawns. The only foreigners were a few Asian kids who stuck closely together. The white kids didn't hang out with the black kids. There were lots of long-standing cliques and friend groups, so once again, I did not fit in and I did not belong. Again, I felt all alone. I walked home from school with my sister and her ninth-grade friends and spent most of my free time with my family working on our new house. *Depression* wasn't a word that was uttered in the early '90s, especially not by young adults, but I was drowning in it and hiding it from everyone around me. It was back to crying myself to sleep at night. I felt angry, upset and deeply hurt. But also, yet again, I felt that I really didn't have a choice. That familiar feeling of resignation and helplessness filled me, but I quietly obliged, obeyed and pushed away my feelings. I was raised to respect what my parents said and to honor their decisions. Although it hid in the more acceptable words like *tradition* or *customs* or *culture*—it was the silencing of my own voice. I did not dare to rebel against them. They were everything to me and I could not risk losing them too. I had lost everything else. Again. I delt with it by staying busy and buying into their dream for our family—a new home and land of our own—in order to numb my own pain and silence my broken heart. I missed my Brooklyn life. It was just a smaller reminder of missing my life in Poland but it was the same familiar ache within me I was suppressing and running away from.

The fact that the house we moved into was in terrible shape didn't make life any easier. I was embarrassed by the place we relocated to, especially because it sat among other normal looking homes on the block. Ours was basically a large-sized garden shed with a small hallway, a room with a tiny kitchen, an area to fit a queen bed, and a little bathroom. It sat back at the very end of a property entirely overgrown with weeds. The small unfinished attic could only be accessed by using a painter's ladder and climbing in through a hole in the floor. The ceiling was so low you couldn't stand up straight. Ania and I were told this was going to be a bedroom she and I would share. I was convinced there must have been some sort of misunderstanding.

In the early days in Baldwin, before school even began that fall, we lived under heavy construction. And when I say that, I don't mean that we hired someone to do it. We did the "constructing" ourselves, along with a few of my parents' friends. We put up walls, added hardwood floors, put in a window (my mom sewed the curtains), and installed lights in the attic. For a while we still had to use the ladder to climb upstairs, but eventually something resembling a staircase was built. The ugly twin mattresses from the Brooklyn apartment were placed in the room, without the legs this time, since the space was so small, and Ania and I had a place to sleep. We figured out quickly how to not pee in the middle of the night since neither one of us wanted to go climbing down that ladder to the toilet when it was pitch black. That summer, I learned how to put up two-by-fours, how to install insulation, how to attach sheetrock to framing, how to spackle and tape, sand down and paint walls, how to use a nail gun, an electric screwdriver, and a jackhammer. I also learned how to drink beer as we celebrated our progress with Żywiec, the Polish beer bought in the Polish neighborhood in New York City called Greenpoint. I felt very grown up and competent. I buried my distress about the move, and the house, and the fact I had no friends again by telling myself it didn't matter because I had family and that was all I needed.

The project became an incredible labor of love, a communion of exiles coming together and building a new life in the promised land for themselves. Of course the house was for us, but it united many for a common goal and we all enjoyed each other's company. Polish friends came on weekends with tools, some with skills, others with food, yet others with vodka. (Actually, probably most of them with vodka.) Everyone was happy, helpful, and willing to work hard. All of them remembering that this was why we all came here—the tough journey to the USA—to make dreams like this house a reality. The workdays were long, and they often turned into late-night dinner parties out on the grass (now slightly mowed). American cheeseburgers and Polish beers. I enjoyed being a part of the comradery and having a job to do. It was amazing to work toward a goal that my parents envisioned. It was motivating and inspiring, and it taught me that anything is possible if you dream about it and work for it, even if it was really difficult or deemed crazy by other people. My parents certainly taught me that I could do anything if I wanted it enough and if I was willing to work hard for it, an important lesson! It was extremely rewarding to see our home taking shape and coming together. I found it more fulfilling than my high school experience that year. I isolated myself from kids my age and poured my energy and time into our family and the house project we were all bringing to life. It gave me (and all of us in our family) so much hope and was such a promise of better things to come—if we just stayed strong and persevered. And so we did. When we'd finished the first phase of construction, we tackled the extension, almost tripling the home in size and adding a large garage to its side. We next put on the brand-new roof and poured concrete to create a driveway. All of this was done by our family with the help of our new Polish American friends, none of whom were actually in the construction business with the exception of one architect. Oh, and the Home Depot credit card. God bless America!

To help with the financial strain of construction, we took on a part-time job as a family. We didn't have to worry about Mores eating packages this time, because it was delivering the *Penny Saver* on Sunday mornings. On Saturday nights, the four of us sat together on the floor of our living room while eating pizza and folded the small newspapers that announced local events, included a few articles, and had pages of coupons. We had to stuff them into yellow plastic bags. It was tricky to eat and stuff because the ink on the paper made our hands black and filthy so we took turns with the pizza. Early on Sunday mornings, we drove to the next town over, then walked for a few hours delivering the publications to people's front doors in Rockville Center. We had a map of which homes subscribed to the paper and which ones didn't. My dad had a system that detailed where the car got parked, who did what street, and when to move the car to the next, most logical location for us all to restock the gigantic Ikea bags we carried over our shoulders. We weren't paid big money, but for us every penny counted.

Mores was making friends in his new homeland as well, having decided to continue his habit of exploring the area we resided in, just like in Szczecin. He learned how to jump the fence around our property and went running through our neighbors' front and backyards, sniffing things and taking in the surroundings. When he was gone too long, we would set out to find him, a few of us on foot and Papuś driving the car with the windows open calling "Mores! Mores!" and whistling for the dog. Eventually the escapee would be located, brought back home, and grounded. It was routine. Except for one time, when he got a little too adventurous and ran into a busy highway where he was hit by a car. We had been walking and looking for him when one of us heard either the impact of the hit or the dog crying, maybe it was both. The person who hit him stopped to check on Mores. When we got to the spot, we placed Mores on a blanket, lifted him into the trunk of our station wagon, and took him to a nearby vet. He needed to have hip surgery. It was scary and I was terrified of losing him, but thankfully he recovered and was okay. He continued running away, slightly crooked, for the rest of his life.

The weekends of my senior year of high school on Long Island were filled with construction, cleaning, cooking, *Penny Saver* delivery, and homework. I was also working on sending out college applications, a major process. Each hand-written application had to be accompanied by an individual essay. I spent one entire weekend crying as I attempted to come up with a story about why I was a good candidate for a particular university. My "favorite" pastime—struggling to prove that I am worthy despite the deep-seated conviction that I am not. I birthed a whole narrative telling the tale of my mom and how she came to America for freedom and to give her daughters a chance at a new life and an amazing education. The opening words were, "There was a small girl living in the country of Poland …" I still remember it.

My parents edited the contents of the essay and sent me back upstairs to rewrite time and again. Up and down the "stairs" (that new-and-improved built-in ladder). It seemed like a never-ending process and I kept saying I just couldn't do it. I broke down into helpless and desperate tears at various points over my ugly green typewriter. My fingers hurt. As did my heart, summarizing what I had lived through. But eventually, I finished it. And submitted it. And I got accepted. They were *so* proud, Mamuś and Papuś. I was too. The immigrant-foreigner-refugee pushed through when everything in my body was telling me to give up. I'd find myself in a space of helplessness and hopelessness, and then a new wind swept through, pushing me forth in my fight. It was a battle. It was a war. I was fueled by anger but also by pride and perhaps, under that, knowing I too had a right to the things I was fighting for. The odds were stacked against me, which was so unfair, and I resented being in that situation. Still, knowing that motivated me in a strange way to prove to "them" that I too could do it. And that I could do it even better. I gladly accepted my invitation to be part of the incoming freshman class at Hofstra University that following school year. I couldn't finish Baldwin Senior High School fast enough.

By then my parents were commuting to New York City from Long Island, leaving earlier and coming back later, driving the family car to Queens to park and taking the subway to the city from there. Because I was the oldest, I had more responsibilities at home. Besides the usual chores, and getting dinner started while my parents were on the way home, I was often the translator. Because I'd learned how to write letters, including proper format and polite openings and closings (this was all before email, Google translate, or online templates—what a relief all of those would have been!), I found myself composing letters for my parents. I helped them understand what came in the mail and I wrote replies. Also, because I could speak English well and they felt uncomfortable because of their accents, I talked to the banks, phone and insurance companies, electricity and water providers. I helped to sort out credit cards. I made appointments.

At the time, I was proud of myself that I could handle it and also happy to be able to help them. They were working so hard, such long hours. It felt very grown up and I saw how much I was contributing to the family. In the long run, this created a pattern that I couldn't break for years. But at the time, back in high school, I was happily codependent and naïvely pleased with my work and mature sense of responsibility. Being always busy and working really hard were respected and praised, and I was doing a damn good job at both. I also really clung to our family due to my strong sense of loyalty and, of course, love. Because we had all gone through something so difficult together, it made us even closer than before. Trauma bonds people like superglue. Because it was hard to make friends (again) I hung on to my parents and my sister even more tightly. They were all I had. Although we didn't speak much about the feelings and emotions surrounding our still very recent escape from Poland and immigration to America, it made us a tight-knit unit. The pain of it all bound us to one another, almost interweaving us into one. Without speaking, the others understood the wound. We relied on each other for survival. We needed one another.

Halfway through the school year, I applied for a job at a local McDonald's. I figured it would be easy because I had experience from working there in Brooklyn. I wasn't involved in any of the after-school activities (besides the school musical "My Fair Lady," which was over by then), and I wanted something to do after school besides chores. I also wanted to make my own money to buy clothes and maybe even to meet new people. It turned out to be the best decision! I made new friends and most of my happy memories from high school in Baldwin are with the people I met at this (greasy) place. We spent time together on breaks, then outside of work, and eventually became inseparable and spent every weekend hanging out. This was also the place, and the friend group, where I met my first love, Ian, whom I dated for almost five years. He, along with the rest of the guys we spent time with, finally made me feel normal again— seen, heard, accepted, valued, even loved. They were a huge blessing at a very critical time and filled my life with laughter and lightness again. I was living again, not just surviving.

In May of 1992 I walked in my blue cap and gown down a hot and sunny football field filled with fold-up chairs and screaming parents (including my own!). I received my high school diploma. I was ready to attend Hofstra University in the fall and a fresh new start, one that I chose myself this time. I would study TV production and broadcasting. I grew up around my parents working in this profession and so we figured I would be good at it. My graduation present was a ticket to go to Poland, to go back for the first time in five years. I would get to stay with my aunt and uncle for the summer in Szczecin. The theory my parents had come up with was this: "If she misses it so much, send her back there and let her see that what she is missing isn't all that great and that what she has now is so much better." All of that completely backfired because I had the best time.

We were not American citizens yet, but I could travel with something called the Green Card. It had the words "Resident Alien" written on top in big bold green letters, which I always found hurtful.

It was not a very welcoming suggestion, but it allowed me to travel freely so I was thankful to have it. This little card put me under the protection of the American government while I was waiting to be *naturalized*. This is a fancy way to say that I was eventually going to be granted US citizenship by the US government, which required five years of living in the States (following a legal entry into the country) and then passing a terrifying in-person exam at the INS (Immigration and Naturalization Service). The "Alien" status made it safe for me to enter and leave Poland. My parents, because of their activism against the old government in Poland, still felt threatened to go until they had their US passports. So it was just me, and I couldn't wait to get there! I wrote letters to all the friends I had kept in touch with, listing the phone number for my aunt and uncle's place and my arrival time. I wrote to family members telling them to expect me. I made plans to visit friends in neighboring towns and even planned a camping trip with a few family friends who had kids my age. These friends and relatives hadn't seen me since the day I disappeared. I would tear up at the thought of seeing Dziadziu Ziuk, my grandpa. Although he had come to see us in the US almost every year, each trip took its toll on him as he was getting older. It also was nowhere often enough for me.

I flew KLM airlines wearing a flowered sundress and dragging a brown leather suitcase, the same one we traveled to America with when we left our country. It was only the second time in my life flying transatlantic and the first flight I had ever taken by myself. It felt super cool and so grown up. I was almost eighteen and I felt so free. I made friends on the plane, and we said goodbye as I transferred to my flight to Berlin at the Amsterdam airport. Berlin was (and still is) the closest international airport to my hometown, about a two and a half hour drive. I was finally going back home.

That summer was simply amazing. I was picked up at the airport by my aunt and uncle, and their embraces felt so welcoming and right. I had missed them immensely. I was jet-lagged so I fell asleep on the car ride back but woke up when it was time to cross the border from Germany into Poland. The feeling was hard to put into words. A mixture of grief and longing with fear and excitement flooded me. I was overwhelmed. I tried to hold back tears as I recognized the familiar booths with the red and white barricades and border patrol officers, first the German control then the Polish control. I held my breath and felt my body tighten with the old familiar feeling of fear. This was how we always reentered Poland from our summer vacations, through this very border check point, me always holding my breath. It felt so normal and right on one level and yet so scary and distant on another. Crossing the border wasn't a dangerous thing anymore, but my brain or my body hadn't registered that. Both were reliving the past in that very instant. I was definitely afraid. I was overwhelmed with emotions although the whole process took just a few minutes—a glance at my passport and a nod from the patrol officer. This was when I realized that a lot had changed since I left. No lines. No searches. No interrogative questions. Just a formality, which was far from how it was before. It felt a little strange.

Entering Szczecin was a long-anticipated return for me. I had spent numerous nights and days dreaming of this very moment and I could not believe it was finally happening. We went straight to my grandpa's house. This became the first stop on all our homecomings regardless of how long the trip was or what time we arrived. There I saw a sight that would greet me each and every time, him waiting at the gate of his home. I had no cell phone, so he had no idea when I would get there, but he was always, always waiting outside. I can remember the shirt he wore most of the time—my mom bought it for him while he was in America—a brown-and-white flannel layered with a black, warm insert inside. He would be in gray dress pants and his slippers and his big hands would wave at me and motion for me to hurry up and climb up the stairs. When he held, hugged, and kissed me, each time, he cried and shook. On that first trip back, I went to see him every day.

The hardest part of going back was walking past our old apartment, the place I called home from birth to the day we fled nearly thirteen years later. It was sold to someone else, and I could not get inside the flat but I did walk into the building and up the hallway stairs. The staircase was dirty and smelled like urine, like it always had. I walked in through the front entrance of the complex and then again through the back door. I visited the courtyard of the apartment building looking for old friends, remembering myself playing and riding my bike there. I saw the old World War II bunker in the middle of the courtyard that we always climbed on top of. When I got a little older and a bit more daring, a few of us would sneak flashlights out of the house and climb into the bunker and go down the long hallway. It ended in a huge metal door that was locked with a wheel-like door handle, which we could never open. It was old and rusted. There were rats down there and it smelled of mildew. The whole thing felt exciting and scary at the same time. I remembered this as I stood there, and I cried as memories like this one tugged at my heart. Longing and sadness filled me. I thought about all the times that I had wished to be back where I now stood. I looked up at the windows into our kitchen on the second floor and then again, the bedroom and living room. I noticed the curtains were different and the little window my parents usually kept open in their room was closed. I felt pain and happiness at the same time. I had a strong urge to stand there and yell "Maaa-maaaa! Taaaa-taaaa" the way Ania and I would yell up to the window when we needed something. But only tears came. And a dull ache in my belly. I had to leave. It was too much.

I walked past our street often, retracing my way to school and to
the homes of our relatives, showing up unannounced and ringing
their doorbells. Various family members, always so glad to see me,
would shout my name:

"Marta!"

"Martunia!"

"Martusia!" without making the weird American *r* sound that
always made my name sound like Marda. I was home, where people
knew my name and how to say it right. Something inside of me
settled down.

I roamed the streets of my city nonstop, taking in how much
it had all changed since we left, how much I too had changed! I
left when I was twelve and coming back I was almost an adult. I
would turn eighteen that September. I spent time with family, and
everywhere I went I got a hug, lots of kisses, often with lots of tears.
There were long talks and a home-cooked meal with tea after always!
I ate familiar foods, I went to familiar places, I sat with family who
knew and loved me. I also visited with friends and got reacquainted
with them. I left them as children and found them again as young
men and women. We sat outside drinking beer together, sharing
stories of the past five years. I saw my hometown through new eyes.
Things looked so much smaller than I had remembered. The streets
were more colorful now, and new buildings were springing up with
lighter and more open architecture. It looked so Westernized.
There was even a McDonald's that opened and a Kentucky Fried
Chicken, as well as several American-style malls.

This trip breathed new life and hope into me and was something
I very much needed. Without really understanding it, I felt like I
was where I was supposed to be, in the right place. I felt it in my
very bones. It was natural. Normal. Things made sense. I felt like I
was back where I belonged, where I was understood, where I didn't
have to explain—I just showed up and I was seen—I didn't have

the weight of that thing I carried around, that lack of something, which made me stand out in a negative way. It was like that empty hole in me was filled. I just fit in everywhere I went in Szczecin. And the phone at my aunt and uncle's home did not stop ringing that summer, for me! What a contrast to having to work so hard to be accepted or even noticed, let alone invited, in high school in America. Here people actually wanted to spend time with me and I was wanted everywhere just because I was me. I was home again. At last.

I took several trips around the country by train that summer. I saw family in Warsaw, where my grandpa's brother gave us a tour of the places they both fought together during World War II and the Warsaw Uprising. He showed me where my grandpa was shot and wounded and talked about the battles and dangers in the city at that time. He explained how the two of them, and their two sisters, had survived.

I visited friends and family in Gdańsk by the sea. We went camping in the countryside, in a place we'd often visited as kids. We swam in the lake, went for long walks in the forest, played cards, read books. At night, we roasted sausages and cooked potatoes in the fire, covered ourselves up with blankets and someone would always play guitar and we'd stay up until the stars lit up the sky above, singing the songs I grew up with. A musical note, a word in a song, a scent, or taste would touch me so deeply, my heart would melt or the longing would come alive and the tears would come. Then we would watch the stars sparkle as we lay on our backs in the grass, my uncle naming the constellations and telling myths and old folklore stories, me always softly weeping. All was well with the world again. All was well with my soul. I vowed at the end of that summer to return every year, and eventually maybe even for good.

# CHAPTER 6

# Fitting In, But Not Belonging

**LONG ISLAND, NY**

**EARLY 1990S**

In September of 1992, I entered Hofstra University as a Communications major. I was excited and nervous, but I felt I could begin again ... *again*. This was my fifth beginning-again since leaving Poland; I thought this time it might stick, that maybe I could finish without an abrupt interruption! I really wanted to believe in that possibility. I reminded myself: "I can do anything!"

Navigating the school campus was intimidating at first, but every other first-year student was dealing with it too, and after a week it was easy. I spent my mornings at school and evenings and weekends working and helping with construction on our house when I could. In addition to keeping my job at McDonald's (because it kept me close to my friend group there), I started a new job at a Hallmark Cards store at the Roosevelt Field Mall close to Hofstra. By the second semester, I figured out that scheduling my classes on Monday, Wednesday, and Friday gave me four full days to work each week. So I added a third job as a sales person at a clothing store called Express at the same mall. I was excited at the discounts it offered and was finally able to purchase nice clothes for myself, which made me feel good.

Since we could not afford housing on campus, I was a commuter student and drove to school from Baldwin in a beige Peugeot (probably to stick with my dad's love for French cars). It was a diesel. This meant three things (to me): First, you could hear me coming from several blocks away, the engine was that loud. Second, I needed to find gas stations which actually sold diesel gas. And third, when it got really cold outside, the car sometimes would just not start. Now let me just clarify right here that I am no expert on cars or engines. Maybe other diesel cars start just fine in the winter. Maybe this was another fixer-upper and therefore slightly flawed. (This obviously is a theme with cars and houses in my family!) The first few weeks of the fall were fine. Once December hit and the temperatures dropped, though, the car would not cooperate. Sometimes I could get a ride with a friend; other times I could scrape up money for a last-minute taxi. More often, and worse yet, I had to take two buses, transferring at the Greyhound bus station in Hempstead and of course arriving late. Long Island public transportation, specifically Hempstead buses, were not the same as what I experienced in Brooklyn, where everyone took buses or the metro. In Long Island, everyone drove. So being on those buses and in that Greyhound station was not fun (or safe). A "character-building" experience, as they say. *It sucked* is how I would put it.

In addition to spending time with my Baldwin McDonald's friends, I started meeting new people in classes and participating in activities on campus and the local college bars. This made for a huge change in my social life, and I finally had an abundance of events to choose from on Friday nights and weekends after work. The days of making up stories at Baldwin Senior High that I had plans with my Brooklyn friends (only to go home and work on the house and fold newspapers into plastic bags) were over. The time spent writing letters to friends back in Poland or Brooklyn or pen pals (new friends felt safer on paper rather than in person) had ended. I was keeping busy and felt fulfilled because I had a lot going on: busy was happy. Life was suddenly exciting and fun and I experienced a sense of freedom being able to come and go even though I was still living at home. Truthfully, I was based out of my car, only returning home to sleep when I wasn't crashing with friends in their dorms at college.

By this time, I had fully taken on the American culture as my own. Most of the people I was spending time with had no idea where I came from or what I had gone through. By not sharing that story, I finally didn't stand out and wasn't different from the others. At last, I had accomplished my goal. It wasn't that complicated to pull off anymore, because the plight of a political refugee escaping communism as a child wasn't something that casually came up in a happy hour conversation. I learned the language, lost my accent, and closed the door on that part of myself, which made life easier. When I slowed down just a little, that longing for home and the emptiness of the gaping hole within were still right there. And the pain and sadness, so much pain and sadness! So then I put several heavy locks on the door and threw away the keys. And I stayed busy to keep from thinking about the door, the locks, and what was behind it.

It worked very well almost all the time. Sometimes, at home, I was required to be someone else, not this new personality I had created for myself and the outside world. I struggled with this then, and for a very long time—and I imagine many immigrants do. I was not really American. When I was with my American friends, I pretended. I was not really Polish either when I was with my Polish family. That didn't really feel comfortable anymore. I was a little bit of both and therefore not fully either one. Although my parents would remind me about getting to pick the best of the two cultures, sometimes I felt like they wanted to do the picking for me. There really wasn't a safe space to explore what my own version of Polish American looked like. And I can't deny that if there was space, I probably wouldn't have been able to navigate it very well. It was so complex and painful and I was so young. When one time I expressed some of my deep frustrations around the topic to my parents, I was told I was being "so American" and the conversation was over. I couldn't help but wonder why we came to America if they didn't want me to become "so American" at least in some ways—like the fact that this happened was somehow an unexpected surprise. But it confirmed what I had been feeling in terms of what was expected of me. At all cost, stay true to the Polish blood running through your veins and be proud of your heritage. But it was impossible to reconcile being proud of my Polishness with my life in American college, which I started to love. I just wanted to have a good time, be free of that weight on my shoulders, and feel like I'd found my people, that things were finally *okay* and life was finally *normal*. I wanted to be a regular young adult and to finally drop this heavy baggage I always seemed to carry along. This thing that was being asked of me by my parents robbed me of the joy I was experiencing with my friends. So I faked it—trying to be all things to all people—and somehow kept my sanity. People pleasing and meeting expectations, however unreasonable they were. It was easier than explaining any of what was actually going on inside of me. Plus, I no longer had the Polish vocabulary to verbalize those things. I stopped learning my native language at twelve—the vocabulary of a sixth grader isn't sufficient to describe the complicated layers of the inner struggle I was experiencing. And explaining any of this in English to my parents always led to huge misunderstandings as their language knowledge wasn't yet developed enough for a serious discussion. It became hard to be able to communicate within our own family on these topics. Or maybe that was just how I justified the fact that we never really talked about emotions and our own internal experience. Either way, not being able to share any of this with my peers or my parents, I stuffed it all and just kept going, just kept juggling, just kept running fast and ignoring my feelings. Surviving the immigrant experience by escaping any remembrance of it. It seemed to guarantee me belonging, so I made the trade only to pay for it much later in life.

In the spring semester of my freshman year, I got an internship at Private Financial Network, thanks to my dad who worked there. PFN was a production and broadcasting company, owned by CNBC, which covered financial conferences and replayed them to their subscription members. This was all before streaming and before the internet! I started as a production assistant and moved my way up to sound engineer, working alongside my dad who was the crew chief and camera operator. He taught me all he knew after his thirty years in the TV business and I was a superfast learner. The company quickly offered me a job, so by the time I started taking communications and production classes in college, I was working as a freelancer making $150 per day. I felt super rich! Since McDonald's paid $3.25 an hour, it was easy to make the choice: I quit all my other jobs and was officially working in the field of my major by the end of the first year of my studies. I loved working with Papuś and we traveled all over the United States as a production team—Chicago, Austin, Minneapolis, Milwaukee, Vail, San Francisco, and Las Vegas to name a few. It was a really amazing and wonderful experience, and I felt very close to and thankful for my dad. We made things happen together. He was really excellent at problem solving, thinking on his feet, and taught me a lot of those skills during our time working out in the field. Solving technical problems at work only prepared me for dealing with issues in real life, thinking outside the box and always finding a way to pull things off. Besides traveling to many new cities all over America and getting to explore them after work (which I loved because we got put up in nice hotels and it felt like such a luxury), a lot of our time was spent at investment conferences in Manhattan and around Wall Street, which I also enjoyed. They were usually hosted in fancy conference rooms in high-end hotels, and I just felt so lucky to be able to be inside of places like that. I also loved Manhattan and learned to navigate it quickly. The city that kicked my ass upon our arrival definitely felt like home to me by now. I loved it. I was a New Yorker! And working there was so exciting. At nineteen years old I was the youngest team member at PFN and also the only woman.

During one of these work trips, one to Las Vegas, at the end of a typically long day, we got a phone call. My dad and I had worked for over ten hours straight and I had just gotten out of the shower when the hotel room phone rang. It was my mom and my grandpa, who was visiting us in Baldwin. They were both hysterical and could hardly speak. All I could understand was Dziadziu Ziuk saying over and over, "My son. Andrzej, my son."

My favorite uncle, my mom's only brother, the one I stayed with during the summer, had tragically died in a drowning accident while on vacation in Spain. My dad and I were devastated. We immediately flew back to New York and joined the rest of the family in mourning. Watching my beloved grandpa grieve the loss of his only son was the hardest of all. He spent days curled up in a ball on my parents' bed just crying. He would lay there in the fetal position, his knees curled up close to his chest, one hand over his forehead and face to hide the tears. "We are not supposed to outlive our children," he would say over and over, and then he would cry again. My mom's brother had come out to visit us once in the tiny Baldwin house. A black-and-white photo of him hung on one of the walls—he was pointing to the stake point in the ground where the house extension would end, my mom leaning over him smiling broadly—taken during this only trip to America. Witnessing my grandfather grieve was terrible, and the loss was very hard on me too. Wujek Andrzej called me his "córeczka" (little daughter). I had a hard time functioning in classes and at work for a while.

Soon after Andrzej's tragic death came another crisis. I woke up one morning to a strange sound coming from the kitchen downstairs. It was almost like a whisper, but how could a whisper possibly wake me? The whispering seemed to be calling my name. I rolled out of bed and stuck my head out the hole of the attic floor to see my mother lying on the floor by the refrigerator, phone in one hand, dressed in her office clothes. I slid down the stairs in what seemed like a second and once I was by her side heard her repeating, "Call 911. Call 911."

I let out a scream, which woke my grandpa, who came running from the bedroom next door in his pajamas. Taking in the scene in front of him, he raised both his hands to hold his head. He stood there frozen, completely in shock, fear clearly visible on his face, looking like a little, helpless, overwhelmed child. Even as this registered with me, I was on the phone with the hospital, managing the drama as it unfolded.

I helped the emergency workers load my mom into the ambulance when it came while comforting her and then helped my grandpa into the car so we could follow behind. The whole drive over I was translating and explaining to him what had happened and what was said. He was still in shock from learning about the death of his son and was now witnessing his only living child, his daughter, being carried away to the emergency room in a foreign, unfamiliar country. My heart broke for him but I was also scared for my mom. I called my dad at the office and he immediately left work for the hospital. I rang the high school office to get news to Ania.

This was a role I learned to play really well, putting my feelings and emotions on hold while navigating a crisis. I would almost take a step back from the situation and absorb, observe, and take it in really quickly like an assessment, never freaking out or losing my cool, my mind racing as I was processing and planning, not getting swept up in the gravity of it or hysteria around me. This all happened very fast. In my mind, I broke things down into smaller projects, pieces, and steps and could clearly see what needed to get done and where we were going. I was a caretaker, fixer, and leader at heart so a solution was already conceptualized and I clearly saw where I was steering the ship, even if it was sinking. Delegating some, but taking on most of the tasks myself, I could direct this orchestra of catastrophe at hand with grace and ease. Whatever big drama was unfolding (and quite a few came!), I was always the calm, cool, and collected voice of reason, a source of comfort and leadership for others. This ability stayed with me well into my adulthood and was a superpower I relied on frequently in life, in college, at work, and while running a company later in life. It came in handy with family as well, especially once my own two children were born and there was a lot to juggle again—the kids, the marriage, the parents, the house, our own business. I would become "command central" for when things would fall apart or into pieces, not just at home but with friends, at school, at work. It became who I was. No wonder that I ended up working for live news for over a decade. Chaos felt like being in a natural environment to me. I would think fast and perform well under pressure and was not afraid to take action. I could also manage several situations and tasks at once, which would earn me the nickname "Super Marta." Breaking news was like breathing air for me. I loved the drama and last-minute deadlines. I thrived in that environment. It was exciting. I just didn't understand that it wasn't healthy and that it was rooted in early childhood trauma and how I managed to cope with it. It was me living out of my stress response constantly. But the adrenaline felt thrilling so I loved it—it was addicting. And people praised me for it and leaned on me, which felt satisfying and rewarding, perhaps even in some way resembled the love and acceptance I was always trying to earn from those around me. I felt needed and that fulfilled me. It gave me a purpose.

My mom came home from the hospital and recovered. She had suffered a ministroke and was told to quit smoking and had to pay special attention to her blood: she learned that she had a clotting disorder. The stress of immigration and the struggles of adapting in a new country only added to the strain on her body and health. She saw a few specialists and was placed on several medications.

We slowly recovered as a family too. Suffering another shock together was so familiar. It almost felt like the most comfortable way we could relate to each other. Things fell back into place and life continued, my mom working for the International Rescue Committee (the organization that sponsored us as refugees from Poland) and my dad working for PFN and CNBC (with me tagging along when I got booked) and Ania continuing at Baldwin Senior High School. Mores was also still around, getting grayer and older, but nonetheless still attempting to run away from home as often as he could. The car accident and broken hip didn't teach him a thing. He was wild at heart, always escaping to search for his freedom.

————————————

Although I loved college life and the career I had started, each summer after classes ended and school was over, I went back to Europe. It called me. I loved being there. It filled a need that went well beyond keeping the promise to myself the summer after high school graduation to go back to Poland the following year. After freshman year at Hofstra, my younger sister and I set off for our homeland together and reexplored the country. She was only nine when we fled and was now coming back at fifteen. We landed in Warsaw this time, and visited family and friends there. We made several trips that summer, one of them to Kraków for the first time. It was beautiful. One of my favorite things about old European cities are the stunning old town squares. Cracow (Kraków) and Warsaw (Warszawa) have plenty of them. Ania and I would sit with family friends and just enjoy the views, the company, the conversations, the passersby, and the people-watching. We would hear about the latest happenings in Poland and share our life experiences in the United States.

From time to time, I felt a painful longing and a calling to something deep within. I'm not sure it was like this for my sister, but for me, each visit back to Poland stirred me up, created a lot of conflict and confusion that I didn't really understand. It was a complicated landscape of emotions. Looking back, I can understand that who I had been as a child was not congruent with who I had become in my early adulthood. Those two iterations of Marta were so different! That difference caused tension and disconnection, almost like an internal split. I also held unexplored loss, grief, and longing for the childlike life in a familiar place, which ended so abruptly. I had no smooth transition over into my teenage years, no integration into my American self. One wasn't born of the other. Rather, one ended and the other began. One was abandoned while the other came in and took over. That's how I had coped with what happened. I shut the door on one and opened it to the next. And so, anytime I heard an old Polish song, saw photos of places I loved, or was with the people I cared about back there—anytime my senses were stirred and reminded of the old familiar with smells, sights, flavors, sounds—the longing came for me, the empty hole inside reminded me that it was still there, and tears would flow like rivers. These trips were a blessing and a curse at the same time because they awakened all this within me, which was unsettling, but they also reminded me that there was more. There was more to this newer American me than what was on the surface. She had depth that was not to be forgotten or overlooked. These reminders would pop in and out of my life until I was ready to really sit with them and listen to what they were saying. It would be years later, in Paris of all places.

That summer, we spent most of our time in Szczecin, our hometown, with never-ending visits to family and friends, which we loved. We shared Polish meals with our aunts and uncles, had teatime with cousins and friends. We played cards with relatives and shared photos of what our life in America looked like, often bringing gifts to each person of items still not yet available in the Polish stores (mostly expensive alcohol from my parents and fancy chocolates for the kids). We sat with our grandpa every day—more conversations and always more tea—and sometimes helped him in his garden, as he was getting older and unable to tend to some things himself. I also got to show Ania around the "new" aspects of our city and how it had changed, but mainly we visited the old places we remembered, which brought us comfort and soothed our aching hearts (although maybe it was just mine that was still aching). We ate our favorite ice cream, candy, and gum, like the two little kids left unattended. We visited our old elementary school, church, apartment (just from the outside again), and playgrounds we'd spent time in. We walked the old neighborhoods hoping to run into old mates, and sometimes we did. It was a special trip and it was extra special getting to experience this return together as sisters. This time, I didn't make her run across the bedroom floor between our beds telling her that it was the ocean filled with sharks trying to eat her.

Back at Hofstra, the highlight of my social life and the reason I finally felt a sense of community came when I pledged a sorority. I didn't even know what one was or that they existed before I entered university. But in the second year of my collegiate career, I found myself surrounded by a group of amazing women and I wanted in. Pledging was a strange concept and quite abusive and unloving, but I simply accepted it as a part of those rules I didn't understand but needed to follow in order to fit in. The girls never circled our fat or made us drink beer until we threw up, as was rumored, but plenty of humiliating things took place in order to get initiated. Somehow we became best friends with the girls who had been yelling and hating/hazing us for several weeks after "Hell Night" was over. We were now *members* and not *pledges* and therefore fully human beings. Some things, I realized, I would just never comprehend about America. (A close second to pledging was American football.) But I suffered through it while studying and working. If others could do it, so could I. "Greek Life" was a really hard concept to explain to my parents. It was so strange to them and I had no words for some of the things taking place. I also was probably embarrassed to share what I was willing to put myself through just to join "a club." And why were there Greek letters involved when it had nothing to do with Greece? I wasn't too sure about that myself. It was just important that I finish what I'd started. I was sleep deprived and stressed so I really didn't want to talk about it. I would hide out in my boyfriend's house anytime I had free hours in my day, and take uninterrupted naps in between classes, work, and pledging events! Nonetheless, the friendships I made in Phi Sig stayed with me beyond college years. My new "sisters" embraced me, welcomed me in, and became family. We had amazing times not just throwing parties and raising money for charity—there were Spring Break trips and life together with NYC as our playground. The one place I always felt home in America was New York City because I was always surrounded by other foreigners. The energy of the city was intoxicating and made me feel like anything was possible, for me. If any place in America is the "Melting Pot" I was promised as a refugee, it is the Big Apple.

I spent the summer after my sophomore year studying in Spain. I had dreamed of going to university in Europe for at least a semester—I almost applied to the American University in Paris instead of Hofstra but they didn't offer the major I decided to study—but once work and sorority life got going, I quickly forgot about that plan. Summer in Madrid seemed like a good compromise and so I was placed with a local host family and enrolled in two classes. Spanish conversation and art history, which took place in the Prado Museum, one of the greatest museums in the world. As I studied Spanish art in the Spanish language in this incredible space, I was simply overwhelmed with the beauty before me, not only the art but also the architecture of the building itself. I absorbed it all like a sponge. I loved learning to navigate a new city, new culture, new cuisine, new language, new way of living, and all the walking and exploring.

We had a great time together with the whole group going out for drinks, dancing, exploring the Madrid nightlife, and also strolling around the streets of the city for hours during the day (studying only rarely and when absolutely required, which meant just before the exams). Weekends were spent visiting various cities in Spain and participating in tours led by our teachers, learning history and art, which were later to be reported on in Spanish in class or in written assignments. What made the trip even more special was that I met an American guy who had traveled to Europe, was studying Spanish and appreciated foreign cultures! The summer romance only added sparkle to the already magical experience and reminded me yet again how much I missed living this kind of life daily: being in ancient cities filled with history, rich culture, and around foreign languages just felt like home to me. The final weekend of the semester was open for personal exploration in Europe, and I knew there was just one place that could be for me, Paris.

David, my summer love, and I made our way to meet up with a couple of my sorority sisters who were visiting the French capital. It was my first time in the City of Light on my own and I was absolutely head over heels. I had been there before several times with my parents as a child so I already had developed a connection with French culture and the love of French cuisine and its melodic, romantic language, which sounded like a love song. That weekend we drank French wine, ate stinky French cheese with warm baguettes, stayed out way too late, and explored the party scene of the city. We spent hours one night looking for a bar called No Name Bar, which one of my friends heard was amazing, only to realize hours later that it was simply a bar with no name above it in the Bastille area of Paris. We stayed out all night and rode the metro back to the hotel in the morning giggling like five-year-olds. It was the most beautiful place I had ever visited. I loved the people, the food, the language, and the way of life there. The architecture was breathtaking. Just walking the streets was an adventure in itself, getting lost in each arrondissement. At each corner you'd turn and stumble onto something more beautiful than the corner before. And the fashion! French women were (and still are!) so elegant, chic, and stylish. I wanted to be one of them. I was hooked. I had always wanted to take French in high school but my mom said that Spanish was more practical to know being in America (it's so close to Mexico, I think, was the argument). And so I stuck with that and never expected that it would be Spanish (and studying it abroad) that would bring me to France! My passion for Paris and love of all things French deepened during that fun, long weekend. Little did I know that twenty years later I would be back in the art and fashion capital of the world, living there full-time!

Junior year flew by and I continued working as a freelancer in NYC and studying full-time while being very active in the sorority's leadership and the broadcasting school. The money I was making not only helped me to pay for college tuition but also allowed for my summers in Europe. Since I partied hard (I was teaching everyone how much vodka Polish people can drink and took my job seriously), it also helped fund expensive cocktails and cover charges while out in clubs and bars in Manhattan. Among all the parties, working, and studying, I finally met a friend who

I considered a soul sister, a true best friend. I always believed you could only have *one* best friend, the word *best* implying that some-*one*-thing is better than everything else. I found the American idea of having multiple best friends very confusing for a long time until I just learned to accept it. But this friend was my bestie, my one. Katerina was an exchange student at Hofstra from Greece, and it was the first time I met another newly arrived foreigner since coming to America. I had finally found someone with whom I could share that side of me that others couldn't really understand. It was our non-belonging that bonded us to each other, our "foreignness." I also was desperate to share some of the early days in my New York journey to spare my friend the pain I suffered while a newbie in the USA. I took her under my wing, told her everything, and we became inseparable. Since my sister Ania had just left for college in Colorado that year, I convinced my parents to let my new BFF move in with us, since she was having trouble affording living in the college dorms. Katerina joined me in the attic of the small Baldwin house, which was now medium-sized.

That summer, my last one before graduation, I decided to go home with my best friend to Greece. We had no agenda but to explore the country together, to lie out in the sun during the day and have a few drinks in the afternoon and maybe meet some cute Greek boys. We spent most of our time with her family in their hometown, but also visited some of the islands and neighboring cities as well as the capital, Athens. It was an amazing summer experiencing yet another new culture and the way of living in it. My family had come to Greece many times as tourists during our summers while still in Poland, but now I got to see life there from a local's point of view. I loved the warm climate, the kind people, the Mediterranean food, and even started picking up the language a bit. Till this day I can read Greek—just don't ask me what I'm pronouncing! We lay out by the pool, walked to the city center to sit for hours just chatting and having cold Greek coffee called *frappe*, cooked and ate lunch with her family at home, took siestas, and went out at night, dinner and Greek dancing. I loved it. I fell in love with a Greek boy who spoke no English and explored Greek villages and islands with Katerina. Everything was so affordable, beautiful, and filled with color. The stunning deep-blue sea, the precious white houses, and the constant heat of the sun and the warm summer breeze—it was another picture-perfect summer. And again, it was a reminder of that deep something within me that wanted to be in these places, that felt at home there. It was like with every trip to Europe there came a big exhale of relief and a slowing down and arriving, perhaps a freedom not to pretend or keep up with the others, but an invitation to just be as I was. Somehow I was okay being a foreigner in these places. Foreigners were everywhere in Europe and it wasn't something they tried to hide from each other. Here, sharing that I was from Poland was easy because people were familiar with the country, and that piece of information could be easily received rather than stir up strange reactions. I didn't have to answer questions like "Is that where polar bears come from?" (yes, someone actually asked me that) or hear that someone was related to me because he once ate Polish sausage and knew it was called *kiełbasa*. I did not have to hear statements like "Go back where you came from!" which always hurt so much and was delivered with a side of anger and disgust. Somehow it felt like being a foreigner in these foreign countries added up to belonging to a bigger whole. The pressure to become like the others, to blend in, which I felt as an immigrant woman in America, simply wasn't present in Europe, to me. Even if some of this pressure was self-inflicted, one can only take so much of being called a "dumb Polak" until she does everything she possibly can to hide that "Polak" part of herself not to get made fun of. In Europe, I felt free and whole because I could embrace all parts of myself.

Not just those that perfectly fit. In America I felt like I needed to become American to be fully accepted.

I headed back to New York making a stop-over in London. I had saved enough money to get a ticket that allowed me two days to explore the city I had never been to before. I stayed in a cheap hostel and toured the home of Parliament and Big Ben on a red double-decker bus. It was my first time in the United Kingdom, complete with fish and chips at a pub and a pint of the local beer. I loved it. I strolled around the city and explored, taking it all in. That's always my favorite thing to do when I arrive in a new place, order a coffee in a local café and just sit and take it all in. I watch the people, their ways of doing life, their body language, their facial expressions, the way they communicate with each other. I listen to the language, the things they say, and how they say them. I observe. I breathe it all in. I feel the energy of the place I am in. I take in the pace of life there. I look at the buildings, the streets, the restaurants, the shops, watching how it all functions. I walk the place till my feet hurt, all day, with no destination in mind. I just like to wander and wonder, pop into churches, shops, local museums. My second favorite thing is a bit less obvious and touristy. I love entering the local grocery stores and seeing what people buy. What does milk look like there? And butter? Bread? What fruit or vegetables are available? What food is sold and advertised? What do people buy for dinner? Maybe I'm testing the place as a potential spot to live? Maybe I'm looking at all this asking myself, *Could I see myself living here? Could this be home? Is this it?* Who knows. I call it exploring. It is one of my favorite things to do, going on such adventures.

Senior year at Hofstra, my Advanced TV Production class teacher recommended me for a new job. A local all-sports television station was launching in nearby Port Washington. I was interviewed and hired, along with a few other students from Hofstra's School of Communications, and my position rotated between teleprompter operator, camera person, and stage manager. It was easy to get the job because I already had a couple years of experience. I was happy about how things were panning out for me. I was set to graduate from Hofstra with a Bachelor of Arts Degree in Communications and was doing well in my classes; I was having fun hanging out and partying with my sorority sisters at Phi Sig; I was working and getting paid well in the industry that I was studying; and I was traveling as much as I could in my free time. My life seemed to be really falling into place and I was happy and busy doing what I loved. While doing Spanish homework behind camera #1 of the studio, I started dreaming, planning, and looking for a job in Spain for an American TV station like CNN. I wanted to meet up with Katerina, who had already gone back to Greece and wanted to be a journalist. We'd somehow both live this wild and free life together taking our American experience and merging it with our European roots to create something amazing. I wasn't sure what that would be or what it would look like, but I knew it would be an incredible adventure. I wanted to somehow bring together the two persons I had been being—the Marta in America and the Marta in Europe—which became so confusing and conflicting at times. I wanted to explore what all of this meant and to investigate that deep longing and pain that stirred up within me when I went back to my continent of birth. Why all the tears? Why so much sadness and pain? I had learned how to really live the celebratory and exciting parts of my life fully. I was always up to something fun or planning an exciting adventure for myself or a group of friends. I loved this about myself, this thirst to explore and discover life. But I also spent most of the school year running from the other stuff, the stuff that would come up during summers in Europe. I hid this part of me from my friends, maybe because I was ashamed of it or embarrassed by it, or maybe because it just simply didn't make sense to me yet. It also hurt so much ... But I wanted to explore this tension inside of myself. I wanted to understand it better. I felt a kind of invitation to something deeper, a search for answers that I needed. Perhaps the tears held some clues? I was curious. Maybe what I hoped to find most of all, but didn't realize, was myself.

---

Despite my perfect plans for life abroad, what happened next entirely changed the course of my life. I didn't see it coming, not even for a second. I fell deeply in love. I met my "one," and together with our drive to succeed, hunger for life and a good time, curiosity about the world out there, and a love for breaking the rules, we took on everyone and everything that stood in our way. In the beginning that meant mainly the local bars and all the people who told us we shouldn't be together. The world was at our fingertips and the plans and possibilities for our future were limitless. I had finally found my belonging, a true companion who saw all of me deeply and appreciated that which made me stand out. He loved me *because* I was different, not *despite* it.

And so the last of my "college summers" was a slightly different European experience, as my two worlds finally collided. This time, I brought along my "American love," Jim, to share the other side of myself (and also my continent) more fully. We packed our bags and headed to Italy and Greece for six weeks—no plans; no agenda; no hotels booked—just letting the adventure unfold before us. We had both been laid off from work because the TV station where we met folded, and we took our severance pay and traveled.

Jim and I flew into Rome and took a local train down to Brindisi, a port town in the south of Italy (I don't recommend this eight-hour journey, but we were on a budget!), and then hopped on a ferry over to Greece (also long and painful *but* inexpensive). We met up with Katerina and spent a few days discovering the ancient city of Athens together. We spent most of the summer bumming around the Greek Islands, just the two of us with a small backpack each. We'd arrive on an island, explore all it had to offer on an old rented scooter, and then, depending on how big it was and how many days we needed to take it all in, we'd decide one morning to check out the ferry schedule for the day and think about where to go next. We roamed around like this from Paros to Antiparos to Naxos, Ios, Delos, Santorini, and Mykonos, sometimes sleeping in hotels and sometimes sleeping on the beach and always enjoying the drinks and meeting fellow travelers. We ate lots of Greek salad, feta cheese, spinach pies, lamb, fish, and local pastries. We explored Corfu before taking a ferry back to Italy and finished up our six week summer tour back in Rome. There we ate more amazing food (all the pasta, pizza, melon with prosciutto, the gelato), drank Italian wine, and saw all the sights and tourist attractions. That was our first summer together, Jim's initiation into my European roots and passion for exploring life in foreign countries. He did well. It was crazy and chaotic. We laughed constantly. And we both loved it. He joined me in imagining ourselves living in all these places we discovered for the first time together. I was surprised that he even seriously considered it, being an American, but it gave me hope that all of what I wanted was possible.

Once we ran out of our severance pay, we returned to the United States to start a new life together, my plans to go back to Europe permanently delayed by a new kind of "home" I had encountered, with the man I loved. Home was where he was; home was this new "us." Perhaps together we could create the kind of belonging that would fill the deep wound, longing, and emptiness within me. I loved him with my entire heart and all of my being. That became the new plan: to be a place of "home" to each other, to belong to one another. We became one, losing ourselves in each other, us against the world.

# External Journey

## PART TWO

# CHAPTER 7

# The American Dream

## BUCKS COUNTY, PA / CARIBBEAN ISLANDS
### 2000—2012

Thirteen years after arriving at JFK airport as a political refu-gee, I was living in a small apartment on the Upper East Side of New York City married to Jim. Marta Kobylińska had become Marta Hobbs and my Polish passport was traded in for the navy-blue American one. Not that I had to give up my citizenship as a Pole to become American—I had dual-citizenship. But I lived my American side preferentially. Wearing her skin was more comfort-able. I embraced her and morphed into what others deemed the more acceptable and lovable one. I became what earned me love and belonging, becoming like everyone else around me. It wasn't forced on me. I chose it for myself. Just like my thirteen-year-old self, still wanting to fit in, I abandoned the foreign parts of myself unknowingly.

I had worked my way through the language challenge and culture shock. I successfully graduated from Hofstra University with my BA in communications / television production and held some really amazing jobs in broadcasting. My most exciting gig was freelance work for a mystery man named Barry.

Barry hired staff for all sports teams coming into the tri-state area to play games—NBA basketball, NFL football (by then I had finally figured out how it works), NHL hockey, collegiate teams. you name it. Local sports teams already had their crews in place, but for the out-of-town teams, he was the man to call to hire the entire production team. I loved it because I never knew what I would be doing or where. I would get a call the night before telling me where and when to show up and what my job was. The more often I was available, the more often he called me, so I was available anytime. He had a strange, deep, raspy voice and it was almost like a secret mission, if I chose to accept it.

"Marta, it's Barry. Eight a.m. call time at Madison Square Garden. Stage Manager. Please confirm. Thank you."

I never met Barry or even saw him in person. I was paid $250 per day and got to play around as assistant director, graphics operator, stage manager, camera person and watch live games. It was easy work and I wanted to be Barry's go-to person for everything. My rule was basically to take any job he threw my way and just figure out how to do it. How hard could it be?! Most of the time I was able to pull it off. I think fast on my feet, learn quickly, and common sense goes a long way, plus I had an excellent education and overview of all the possible positions in a production team.

*If that guy can do it, so can I!* was my line of thinking.

Well, I did get myself in some hot water once, when I was hired to run graphics for a live basketball game. I showed up at the broadcasting truck and realized that I did not know the specific equipment I was hired to operate. I sat there trying to master it (good thing about showing up early) and not to panic (this was before the days of being able to look it up on YouTube), when it was suddenly announced that the game was canceled at the last minute. An hour of stress and a full day's pay! I got so lucky! You'd think I'd have learned my lesson, but I didn't. I still thought I could figure anything out myself, fake it till I mastered it, and then beat others at it. There was something so exciting about it but at the same time so scary. I fed off the adrenaline rush of it all. It was probably my immigration experience playing itself out over and over again: sink or swim, do or die, learning new things on the fly as if my life depended on it. I have to say I got quite a few jobs this way but thankfully I never had to work graphics again. I took every job Barry called me in for, and this really built up my résumé and network of connections in the TV business, which led me to landing my dream job by the time I was twenty-five. But more on that later.

Jim and I were engaged in Paris, France; married in Szczecin, Poland; honeymooned in Santorini, Greece. I felt like he really saw me for who I was and celebrated that about me. He proposed to me in my favorite place in the world, the city of love, Paris. Our wedding took place not only in my hometown, with my whole family present, but in the cathedral where I was baptized and had my First Communion. Of course, Dziadziu Ziuk, the patriarch of the family, was the guest of honor and gave our union a special blessing that he wrote and recited himself. He also gave the first toast! Our honeymoon destination was the place where we took our first European trip together, our favorite Greek island. All of it was so thoughtful, intentional, and romantic. I was constantly astonished that someone could pay so much attention to what was important to me and heard and remembered what I said. He made me feel incredibly special and completely swept me off my feet. I knew he was my soulmate, there was simply no doubt about it. We were crazy in love with each other and made an amazing team. While I brought my "I can figure out anything" mentality, Jim lived by "let's have some fun." We were a wild, passionate, and adventurous pair with big dreams for the future.

Jim and I spent a year and a half living in upstate New York, working in television for the CBS affiliate, Jim as weekend sports anchor and me as chief editor for news. This was another job I was hired for simply because I said I could do it, only to train myself over a weekend and start running a whole department on the following Monday. I had some editing experience from a small job, but this was my first exposure to working in live news and I absolutely loved it. It was fun, exciting, and filled with stress, pressure, and last-minute deadlines—the environment in which I thrived. It was basically organized chaos, which was somewhat my normal in life and I was able to be the calm presence who organized, delegated, problem-solved, got things done, and told everyone to "calm the fuck down." (There is a lot of cursing in TV News.)

It was also in snowy Rochester that we welcomed our precious baby girl, Mira, born on October 23, 1998. She was named after my grandma Mirosława (Dziadziu Ziuk's wife, whom I never met but everyone said I looked like), her birth announced live on the six o'clock news by our colleagues at Channel 8. From the beginning, she did not fuss one bit and slept through the night. We were constantly checking if she was breathing! She had a head full of black hair, was the easiest baby ever, and became the center of our universe, teaching us a love we didn't know existed. Mira was always smiling and brought tremendous joy into our life. I simply loved being her mama and immediately knew that motherhood would forever be my most important job on earth.

———

Wanting to be closer to my parents to help us raise our daughter, we left Rochester and headed back to New York City. But perhaps the one winter we spent upstate when six feet of snow fell in less than forty-eight hours may also have had something to do with this decision (not to mention missing the energy and nightlife of NYC—I was 24). Not being able to afford a place of our own in Manhattan, we moved into the "medium-sized" Baldwin house for six months with my mom and dad, sharing that one tiny bathroom among the four adults plus a baby! I didn't think of it as a step backward or a low point in my marriage or life at all. It just made sense that when I needed help, the first place I would seek help was my family. My parents definitely instilled that in me. I felt supported and I treasured having us all together. All the people I loved in one place. It made my heart feel full. Family was everything to me and it felt like ours was growing and I had started to put down some roots. Perhaps all of this was the purpose of the suffering of having left behind the past life, as hard as it was. As our family expanded and I became a wife and a mother, my two cultures seemed to merge as well. It felt like we began weaving something new and beautiful all together. I finally understood what my parents always said about picking the best of both cultures. I got to do that in my marriage and as a parent. Singing Polish lullabies to Mira at bedtime and watching *Sesame Street* in the mornings seemed to be a happy combination. Teaching Jim Polish baby words but also learning from him American terms for pacifiers, bottles of milk, and baby blankets. Mira asked for things in both languages. My parents and I learned from Jim and he learned from us, merging customs of the two cultures into one: our own. I started to find some stability in my identity and who I was at last. Being a wife and a mother was very important, meaningful, and fulfilling. I loved it and it seemed to come naturally—I was a caretaker at heart. The one loving others defined me well as a person.

Jim was a wonderful partner and an amazing father. He also loved my parents, who welcomed him into the family, which was a huge relief for me. I finally started to feel less divided between the two ways of being as it all merged together under one roof in the Baldwin house I once hated so much. We got into a nice groove all together. The house was filled with love—Mira's first spoken words were in Polish and her very first footsteps were taken in the home we had all built together as refugees, not long after arriving in America. Jim and I were broke but happy, and the five of us lived together in a tight space filled with so much joy watching our little munchkin grow. We all adored her. We said goodbye to Mores, who passed away during my pregnancy, and welcomed in a new four-legged family member named Remos (from the letters M-O-R-E-S my dad formed the name R-E-M-O-S). He was my parents' new baby and Mira's first best friend.

————————

My dream job while in college was working for NBC at the infamous 30 Rock building at Rockefeller Center in Manhattan. Thanks to all the connections I made wherever I went, and all the "yeses" to the craziest of jobs, one day I ran into someone I studied with at Hofstra while working as a freelancer for the TV station NY1. He also worked for NBC. Next thing I knew, I was interviewing for a position of video editor for live news at the network. It was a huge accomplishment, just two years after graduating college. The person who interviewed me said they had never seen anyone edit so quickly as she watched my fingers run across the editing console. Coming from someone working in the number one television market in the country, this was a massive compliment. But I knew I was good—people would come to watch me work at other stations. I practiced and worked hard at being the best at my craft. The day I was interviewed, the material I edited during my audition aired on live TV. I cried while watching it at home in Baldwin with my whole family. *I made it!* I thought to myself. I was extremely proud of how far I had come. I was super excited, appreciative and loved everything about my job (okay confession: not the overnight shift, which was required to get my foot in the door) but especially its location. It was so cool to have a pass around my neck with "NBC NEWS" written on it and be able to enter buildings and restricted areas while tourists swarmed all over the place to see the Christmas tree, to ice skate on the skating rink, to see celebrities enter the taping of *Saturday Night Live*, or watch the *Today Show* broadcasts early in the mornings. I loved working in New York City again. While Jim and I commuted from Long Island to work, Mira stayed home with my mom, who just retired from the International Rescue Committee. My dad was working for Bloomberg TV in midtown Manhattan, and my sister Ania was living in Colorado, having graduated college.

Everything seemed to be working according to plan, the new plan, which combined my European roots and my American situation but kept me based in the USA. Jim and I still traveled to Europe in the summer—he knew my relatives in Poland and they met our little Mira once she was born (they called her "Mirunia"). We took time to explore new places together, which I still loved doing. We also both loved to party (this also honored both the cultures!) so everywhere we went, we had a blast and always made tons of new friends. Embracing the American part of myself, I pursued not only some amazing career opportunities but eventually also "the American Dream": striving to become a successful and wealthy entrepreneur. It took dedication, resilience, and some incredibly hard work, but being a refugee taught me how to do all that. I was a master at it actually. It had become my preferred way of not having to deal with any of the grief and pain of immigration: achieving, overcoming challenges, succeeding, pushing through, working hard, and tirelessly. Proving that I was worthy even as an asylum-seeker, I taught myself to believe that I could do anything if I dedicated myself to the task, especially when others doubted me. That was just extra motivation, almost like a dare. There simply wasn't anything I could not learn or figure out for myself if I studied it thoroughly enough. I trusted that. I trusted myself. Jim, in addition to trusting me too (one of the many reasons I loved him so much), brought along his big vision, enthusiasm, desire to have fun, and a finance degree. We were both driven, creative, impulsive and always up for an adventure and breaking the rules. So when in March 1999, my parents gifted us a week in their timeshare in the Caribbean, offering to also watch Mira, it seemed like just a simple couple's getaway. A much needed vacation in the midst of a heavy winter and five months of adjusting to life of working full-time while also caring for a newborn. St. Martin—neither of us had been there before—had sun and beaches, a reputation for great nightlife, and half of it was French! It ticked all the boxes. We were expecting to have fun, which we did. We were not expecting it to be a life-changing experience and the start of something massive we created together. But it was. Game over the minute we set foot on the island. We had found our mission, or rather it found us: to build a business around the Caribbean way of life. We loved the weather, the people, the nature, the lifestyle, the Caribbean vibe, and wanted to start a company that would allow us to come back again and again. We wanted to live "on vacation" all the time and to share it with other people because it was so amazing, and we simply decided "why the hell not?!" The islands were calling! It turned out to be the start of what became a multibillion-dollar company. Everyone thought we were crazy. Most people said we'd be divorced in a year. But the moment someone told either one of us "no," we'd simply respond with, "Oh yeah? Watch this!" And so we built a Caribbean empire. You know, as you do … ;)

On the way back from our second or third trip to St. Martin, we came up with the name "CheapCaribbean," which we wrote on a cocktail napkin of the American Airlines flight home. In December 2000, we registered the URL www.CheapCaribbean. com, which we bought for a mere $9, and began building our first website using a simple template. The main image on our original homepage was a palm tree on a beach with perfectly white sand and beautifully turquoise ocean colors. We found it somewhere online and thought it was pretty, later learning that it was actually not even a photo of the Caribbean but French Polynesia! That's how it all began.

We called ourselves the Caribbean Experts (even though we apparently couldn't tell the Caribbean islands apart from those in the South Pacific!) and started by focusing on selling the one island we knew and loved the most, St. Martin. By the time we launched CC (as we came to call it for two decades that followed) full-time, we had been to the thirty-seven-square-mile island a half a dozen times. We knew all the tips and tricks and had firsthand knowledge, as well as insider advice on the destination. We knew where to find the best pizza, where to get a haircut, where to find the cheapest happy hour, where the best-priced grocery stores were, where to rent a car, which beach is best for various needs in various times of the year. And this became the niche—we knew the island inside and out *and* our enthusiasm for traveling there was simply magnetic. Clients picked up on it and loved it. We not only studied the island religiously, we also made many local friends on the island who could touch base with our customers and help them while they were down there. Pretty soon we had a ton of regulars booking with us and they loved the experience so much, they told their friends. We simply replicated this way of working with other islands and were off to the races.

When new clients thought it was suspicious that we didn't charge taxes, we added 8 percent to our online prices to seem more legit. It worked. When customers thought it was weird that a week in a studio was the same price as a two bedroom, we made up a price scale and up-charged for the larger units, just to seem like we were not a scam. It worked. When people thought it was bizarre that we didn't offer flights to go along with our hotel deals, we started buying them tickets on Expedia to be able to provide a "package" deal. It worked too. Back then everyone was still very leery about making purchases online, especially travel. It was the early days of shopping online and people booked travel by walking into their local travel agency and leaving with printed itineraries and paper airline tickets (people actually paid by checks!). The awesome thing was we were one of the first to disrupt this way of selling travel: groundbreaking, making up the rules, inventing, experimenting, innovating. We loved it. Being one of the first was also a very challenging thing: paving the way for others, overcoming customers' fears that we'd just run with their money and questions about whether or not we were "for real." There were many hurdles to jump over as a start-up dot-com and especially a travel company. It was considered a high-risk business, and simple things like a credit card processor (to charge cards online) were difficult to get approved for. We just tackled one thing at a time, maxed out our credit cards as we grew, personally guaranteed everything, and made it happen. Besides being somewhat naïve about the risks we were taking, a lot of luck was involved in addition to our out-of-the-box thinking, hard work, and the willingness to work around the noes we were often hearing. We worked on CheapCaribbean before and after our regular jobs, during lunch breaks, and on weekends. We were obsessed. We lived and breathed it.

Steady work for us both for six months (me still at the NBC gig in addition to the new hobby of our internet start-up), plus the extra income from a few Caribbean sales a week, allowed us to rent our own place in the Upper East Side of Manhattan, a one bedroom with a tiny little eat-in kitchen that we turned into Mira's room. Jim's new job was located only a few blocks from mine, on Madison Avenue, so we often met for lunch or after-work drinks, depending on my shift. I was really loving life and having a great time—working hard and playing hard, surrounded by love—my daughter, my husband, my parents, my family, new friends, new coworkers, and a job I had dreamed of, New York City, and the Caribbean as my playground.

*This is something books are written about and movies are made of,* I thought often.

I just couldn't believe how amazing life was—after all that heartache, I had finally found my place and my groove. It was more incredible than I could have ever imagined. The little girl in me was beside herself with awe and excitement. I had no clue that something called the Caribbean even existed as a kid. Now I got to visit this paradise land on a regular basis. The immigrant teenager in me who suffered so much through high school never imagined having such a kind, generous, smart, and handsome man by her side who deeply loved her. She never thought being a mother would be so heart-opening and fulfilling and that her little daughter would light up her world. It seemed like I was given all these things after years and years of pain and tears. The depths of darkness I had faced as a child and young woman were now met with the highest of joys and love on the other side of my struggles. It was incredible and unbelievable. So hard to believe that I was actually unable to receive much of it fully, in a truly deep and embodied way. It just didn't seem real. It felt as if a part of my brain couldn't register the remarkable wonderfulness of it all because I hadn't encountered this kind of feeling before. I would pinch myself and it still wouldn't seem real at times. It was so new and unfamiliar. And because it was new and unfamiliar, sometimes in strange ways it felt threatening, fear of the unknown. Sometimes when I let the experience of so much joy and love into my heart, this enormous panic would swoop in: the fear of it being taken away; the fear of losing it; the fear of being back in the dark, sad, and lonely place that I knew so well. Sometimes when I let myself embrace the love and joy, I would start to cry, as a horrible terror of losing them again completely smothered the wonderful feelings.

So I decided with everything within me that I would do what I could to hang on to this "good" way of life for the fear of going back to the "bad" kind. It became a game of survival, needing the highs and excitement and those OMG moments because if they were missing, if they were not there for a moment, that meant I was falling back into the abyss of old pain and sorrow. I was not going back there. Ever. So a new way of existing was born: being the one chasing the highs in life. On the surface, I chased those highs for the pure joy of it, simple love for it, or playing or having fun. But deep inside, I chased those good times as a way to escape the wounds I carried within, a way to avoid ever having to face them. This only ensured, in reality, that no matter how much I achieved or how high the places I'd climb to, it was never enough. What I only learned later is that the hunger of the brokenhearted child within cannot be satiated with external things. Trying to provide enough excitement, money, power, success … always fails. But at the time I didn't know that's what I was trying to do, let alone that it was in vain. All I wanted was to feel good, always be happy, and escape the pain of the past. It worked for a while and it was an amazing ride at the same time.

I was twenty-six. When I looked around me to see what everyone else was doing it seemed they too were in this race. Career, success, wealth, consumption of what was in front of them. Like there was this formula: get married + buy a house + have babies + drive a minivan = live happily ever after. Variations of it included jobs, promotions, and wealth or bigger houses with larger lawns, fancy cars, and never-ending home improvements or larger apartments … But I saw everyone playing this game and we all called it life. So, as I had learned to do while I was young, I observed, figured out the rules, schemed up my own shortcuts, and played along. Actually, when I compared myself to others, I felt like I was winning.

"Time to do more of it, time to do it harder," I decided. "It's working."

I pushed fear down. I buried my wounds. I wiped the tears

when they came until they simply stopped coming. This new "becoming" was my focus. No need for a vision board! I knew I was building the American entrepreneur woman. Yet again, I morphed into what I thought I was supposed to be next. Like a chameleon changing her exterior to match that of her environment to ensure survival and, this time, something much better than survival: success. I could show myself and anyone else who cared to look that I belonged, was welcome, had found my place.

I focused on this new adrenaline rush that our amazing life gave me. Endless good vibes only. It felt so good in my body and in my heart after years of aching and loneliness and despair! I was hooked, addicted, convinced I'd found all the answers. My God, it was such a relief and reprieve from the previous heaviness of life. I completely got lost in the sweetness of it all. I loved life and life was loving me back. This feeling of flying high, achieving the impossible, surprising everyone—most of all myself—with what I could pull off. How amazing could I make it all be? It was hypnotizing and mesmerizing and like a drunkenness of sorts, the kind that makes you feel invincible.

After the first taste of how good it feels to make it, we wanted bigger. We wanted to take over the marketplace and be the best, to tackle the giants in our industry. And crush them. And we were crazy enough to think it was possible. These days they call it *mindset* and *visualizing* and *manifesting*, but back then we were just labeled delusional and even insane. Oh, it was so much fun proving everyone wrong! Our enthusiasm was contagious, and next thing we knew, we were overwhelmed with business and needed to make the riskiest move of all: going "all in" on our vision.

What made it all work was that the goal never was getting rich. What we wanted was to give others the opportunity to experience the same kind of high we were experiencing, by either coming to work for us, coming to do business with us, or booking their next trip with us. Once we tapped into this amazing feeling, which fueled and drove us, we wanted to share it with others. And this was our *why*. We simply wanted to spread the love, the fun, and the joy. We wanted everyone to have access to this experience of life. And any profits we made we wanted to give back, to the Caribbean countries we worked with (later to include also Mexico and South America) and to our employees. We wanted to do all this while being a nonprofit organization and to better the lives of others in some way.

Very soon, CheapCaribbean started to expand rapidly. Once the aftermath of 9/11 settled (which we lived through as Manhattan residents stuck for two weeks in the Cayman Islands), the phone did not stop ringing.

Maybe more people wanted to run from reality just a little bit, to enjoy themselves, to forget the terrorist threat. Maybe the Caribbean—not too far away, no passports required (then)— offered the perfect destination. Maybe many were longing for an all-inclusive getaway to a beautiful beach, turquoise waters, warm sunshine with a little rum punch or a pina colada. An ideal escape. Certainly, the name worked wonders. CheapCaribbean. People understood what we were doing. We loved the islands ourselves and just wanted to share their beauty with as many others as we could by offering amazing deals, passing along the savings, making it possible for everyone to go.

As the company was evolving into its next phase of growth, our season of living in Manhattan came to an end. We loved NYC and took advantage of all it had to offer during our two years on 96th Street and 3rd Avenue, but we were ready for a slower pace and a larger place so we decided to move to Bucks County in Pennsylvania. Our plan was to run CheapCaribbean full-time, but initially with the backup plan of me keeping my freelance work at NBC. I would commute to New York City and continue to work at the TV station.

In January 2002 we loaded up a U-Haul van and drove it to Doylestown, Pennsylvania, to start yet another chapter of our lives together. We bought our first home with a backyard, an extra bedroom, and an office. We convinced Jim's younger brother Mike to move and join us in this crazy CheapCaribbean venture. He came with his dog Kylie and the three of us started really investing all our time, energy, creativity, and resources in the company. For the first four months of that year, I took Mira to Baldwin, New York, on Wednesday mornings. I would then leave her with my mom (in the very same house we built a few years after arriving in America) while I commuted to NYC to work. I would do shifts at NBC Wednesday through Friday (spending nights at my parents') and then drive back to Pennsylvania and help the guys with "CC" Saturday to Tuesday. While I worked at the TV station, in between editing video for the news, I would handle customer emails, send confirmation documents, and charge credit cards. So really it was back to what I knew to do well: working multiple jobs at the same time. I was a mom, a wife, a news editor at NBC, and a business owner/entrepreneur. In my spare time, I cleaned our house (also known as the company headquarters) and cooked us all meals while spending quite a bit of time driving between the states of New York and Pennsylvania. This was the familiar pattern developed and perfected within my own family when we first arrived in America.

By April, only three months later, I had to quit NBC to join Jim and Mike full-time because it started to get that busy. By then, we had twelve phone lines running into our home, the highest capacity internet connection, Blue Cross health insurance for all our employees (initially three people all with the last name Hobbs), and ADP payroll (even though only Mike initially had a salary). We contracted a web design company to help put together a more professional site, designed a new logo from a sketch I drew on a napkin, and started learning about online marketing and advertising. It was also time to move into commercial space and start hiring people who weren't related to us. We ran out of siblings and also friends to bring on the team, and our house was overflowing with people coming in and out all hours of the day for their work shifts. The spare bedroom and the office could fit no more desks, office chairs, and filing cabinets. We blinked and there were forty people working for us and we were moving once more. We blinked again and we became the second largest employer in Bucks County, Pennsylvania. A year and a half later, we moved into our third commercial space taking up 10,000 square feet in a custom-made call center with offices.

As the CheapC family grew, so did ours. I was pregnant with our second baby and we decided to design and build our dream house in a beautiful area of Bucks County. As my belly was getting bigger and bigger, we transitioned the company into a larger office space and started construction on the new house, everything expanding at the same time! It was a dream come true to design and build our new home. Picking out all the details, changing the floor plan to reflect what we wanted, blowing out walls, selecting tiles, colors, wood and stone, doors and windows. I loved every minute of it.

*Not too bad for an immigrant kid from Poland*, I thought, watching the framing go up and the house starting to take shape.

Not too bad, indeed. It looked like a mansion I had only seen on TV. Never ever did I dream something like this could one day be a part of my own life. Again, it felt like a dream. And again, I was pinching myself watching it all unfolding. I remembered the little garden shed in Baldwin becoming a home and understood the pride my parents must have felt at the time. It was their dream. And now I was living out mine while picking stone for the two-story fireplace that would go into my very own living room. It was surreal. It actually wasn't even a dream becoming reality—I didn't even think or imagine that this was possible when I was younger! I'd continue pinching myself over and over and squeal with excitement each time we drove by to check on the construction's progress. Once the floors were down and windows started going in, I cried while walking my parents through it. It was incredibly beautiful and it sat on two acres of land in the best school district in the state.

"I made it," I said to myself, once again.

When I was eight months pregnant, we received the news that Dziadziu Ziuk had died. Because I was so far along in my pregnancy, traveling back to Poland for the funeral was out of the question. I got the news while I was in the car with Jim heading to the office one morning. We had just parked to go inside and start our day. Jim drove me right back home instead where I grieved the loss of my beloved grandpa immensely. I loved him so much. He was almost eighty-nine years old and suffered a rupture of a heart aneurysm. Although I saw him at least once a year and corresponded with him by letters regularly, I always wished he could have been a bigger part of my life. I always missed him. I still do. He did get to see the early days of our company and our first home in Pennsylvania. He met Jim several times and loved him. He spent enough time with Mira for her to remember him and simply adored her. I was very thankful for that. He never got to meet our second baby, our son, who always said that they crossed each other on the way out of and into this world, giving one another a high five. Dziadziu Ziuk died just two weeks before I went into labor.

Andrew James blessed us with his presence on December 1, 2003. AJ, as he quickly became known, made up his own schedule and did not play by the rules from the start. There was no napping at nap time and no sleeping at bed time, regardless of what routines I put in place and tried. He just did his own thing. He ate like a champ and the moment he started walking, it seemed that he was just constantly running and usually laughing and cracking everyone up. He always was, and still is, the center of attention. He couldn't sit still and was active and excited about everything. AJ always kept us on our toes and his sister was super tender with him and extremely protective of her brother. They loved each other from the start—my two most cherished treasures, and all of my heart.

AJ needed a little help in getting used to the frequent traveling and was a bit uncomfortable on planes, reluctant to sit still for long periods of time. I learned this on a 7.5-hour flight to Barbados for my thirtieth birthday, when he was just nine months old. AJ bounced around the whole time on the laps of his mommy and daddy, and also ripped out my earring and threw it somewhere under the seat. However, with a little practice and coaching from his sister (and also *Dora the Explorer* on DVD), we got the hang of it as a family. Jim and I loved bringing the kids on the road with us as often as we could—we hated being apart. Contracting was one of my favorite parts of the business because it allowed me to do one of the things I love the most, travel regularly. I lived in Pennsylvania but had a year-round tan because I was in the Caribbean for work once a month on average. Business suits and flip-flops were my uniform in the office when I wasn't away, rain or shine (or snow!). But getting to go down to the islands to attend trade shows, meeting with hoteliers and tourism partners, and checking out properties was such a fun part of the job. Since we so often traveled with Mira and AJ, our business associates knew our kids too. Our company was who we were, not just as individuals but as a family. Pretty soon we were supporting destinations with our not-for-profit work through the CheapCaribbean Cares Foundation and the company mission officially became "To treat everyone—customers, employees, vendors—like part of the family, while having as much fun as humanly possible." People bought into our vision, believed in what we were building, and wanted to be a part of our team. We genuinely cared about the destinations and ended up making great friends with our vendors, partners, hoteliers, tourism departments, and governmental representatives of the islands. It was these special relationships that fueled the success of it all.

Our employees were truly an extension of our family—our home was about a ten-minute drive from the office and our kids were a constant presence in the call center. At the same time, business meetings often took place at our home. There were really no boundaries or clear lines defining family versus work, no time away. We ran the company working day and night, seven days a week, but also created a culture of community, belonging, and fun around all the hard work. We expected loyalty, reliability, and professionalism and we rewarded it well. We felt that we were building something incredible together with our team and we appreciated each of them. We were very clear about the fact that none of the huge accomplishments that took place would have been possible without the people who contributed to the success of our business. We also felt bonded together by this big vision we were trying to honor; as if we were all on a massive mission together. We worked hard, but we played hard too, as the saying goes. We offered ample vacation time, great health care benefits (including a generous maternity plan, which was very important for me to offer to the ladies at CC since I didn't have one with my first baby), unheard of (back then, anyway) 401K with matching, and access to discounted trips for everyone. We paid extremely well, celebrated everyone's birthdays and weddings, and quite often held a company happy hour in the local bars around Doylestown. Once a year we sent every employee in the company on what was called a Fam Trip, so that they could get to know the destinations and hotels we worked with. We also held a lot of fun events for our staff and I loved planning these. On Valentine's Day, I came in early and left little gifts on each desk in the office before we opened. In the summertime, we hosted a company barbecue at our house, held picnics, and hired the ice cream truck to come to the office during work hours. On Thanksgiving we had over everyone who had no plans (until the company grew too large to do that!) and prepared a feast. Christmas was filled with Ugly Sweater Contests, present exchanges, catered dinners, and seasonal decorations. The annual Christmas parties with a live band, open bar, and a fancy dinner and dancing were my favorites. We attended concerts and race car events together as a company. We participated in a local Philadelphia radio station's food drive to donate food for the homeless and won it several times. This got us to host the radio morning show at our office or, more precisely, in our parking lot under rented tents. It had snowed like crazy the night before and we had rented a dunk tank for "Sink Caribbean Jim." Jim went ahead with it anyway, in a crazy scuba suit so as not to freeze! The second year we decided to take the radio show on location. I chartered a 747 plane and flew all our employees to the Caribbean, along with the WMMR Preston and Steve show and its crew. Did I know how to do this? Had I ever chartered a plane before? Let alone a huge one that size?! Of course not! But I pulled it off—asking the right people the right questions—and it was unforgettable! Interestingly, the plane flew in to St. Martin, the island where it all began. I booked two catamarans and sailed our team (and the radio station folks) over to the island Anguilla for a Jimmy Buffett concert on the beach, complete with T-shirts commemorating the experience. It was amazing.

Pretty soon there were 200 of us in the CC Family with call centers in Doylestown (Pennsylvania), Florida, Arizona, New Jersey, and Boston filled with agents we called "Caribbean Consultants." We implemented a working from home program, which was pretty innovative at the time, and called it the "Phone Home Program."

It allowed us to keep growing without needing more office space. We launched CheapCaribbean in Canada, opened up IT offices in Poland and Vancouver, and expanded into the cruise industry.

Balancing running a large company and being a mom to a kindergartener and a newborn proved to be a challenging task. As business owners and entrepreneurs, Jim and I worked all the time, including late into the nights and through the weekends. Even when we took time away from the office with family, we worked. It was overwhelming at times, but I still always put the kids first every way I could. However, as a mom and business executive, I felt like I was doing neither job very well. What added on even more stress was the fact that I was living with a big secret that started to get too difficult to manage. Kind of like not telling anyone I was a foreigner and failing biology, or pretending the exile from Poland never really took place, or not telling my friends in elementary school that we were escaping. Maybe secrecy was just something that I grew up with and so there were always things I was hiding from others? Maybe it goes back further than I can even remember or know in my family line? The big one that I was hiding—refusing to even be honest about it with myself—was the fact that my kind, fun, generous, and loving husband had a drinking problem.

———————————

Jim was a highly functional alcoholic who was beloved by everyone around us. He was the life of the party and brought joy wherever he went. He was a brilliant leader and a visionary. He was an amazing husband. He was an incredible father. He was my best friend … just not full-time. I opened myself up to him completely and loved him with all of me. Then I came to see that he loved another more: his alcohol. I often felt that I was the only responsible adult in our household, which put a lot on my shoulders. I felt betrayed, abandoned, angry, brokenhearted, and very much alone. I had two children and was running a large business together with my husband who was in active addiction.

The pressure that came with the growing company fueled Jim's drinking. Jim's drinking also fueled his drive to take on the world and push those we worked with—himself most of all—which in turn fueled CheapCaribbean's success. It's hard to say if the business and its explosion would have happened without the addiction. At the time, I wasn't asking myself that question at all. I was conflicted, but absolutely convinced I had to keep up appearances and make sure Jim's drinking and its consequences stayed hidden. It somehow felt like my responsibility to keep everything functioning. I didn't want to lose any of it. This was my life. This was everything.

It was "everything" in more ways than one. I felt tremendously alone at times, extremely happy at others, stressed to the max, worried about Jim's health, proud of his work and creativity, excited and astounded at our accomplishments, scared for our future, afraid for the kids, madly in love with the kids, desperately wanting to help Jim, loving him blindly, hating him when he was in the midst of a drinking binge, or in a post-drinking hangover state. It was all so extremely complex and confusing and heavy. I carried it all, held the tension of all these feelings at the same time, while keeping up appearances to everyone on the outside. Sharing any of it felt like betrayal and I loved Jim and was committed and loyal. That somehow translated into meaning I said nothing. It felt like I was guarding the family and holding it together by keeping this secret. I thought I was the glue, and maybe I was. Putting on a unified-front look for our employees; keeping things calm at home and protecting the kids by keeping the family routines going whether Jim joined us or not; keeping relationships and partnerships functional within the business when he'd drink too much. I felt this was what I was supposed to do because I knew how to do it. I was an expert at managing crises and controlling chaos. I was a fixer. This was my identity.

It felt like putting on masks for the sake of others, and back then I thought that's what love was: loving Jim and loving those I was reassuring that things were still "just fine." But the one person I wasn't loving in all of this was myself. I often felt like I was the punching bag for many, absorbing all kinds of impact and just trying to keep the peace, while nobody was ever really satisfied. It was never enough. I could never do enough and I could never be enough. The reality of trying to keep everyone happy is that everyone simply can't be happy all the time. It was an impossible and unrealistic expectation I set for myself. But I continued cleaning up the messes. Smoothing things over. Explaining. Repairing. Mending. Picking up the slack. Taking on the extra responsibility. I thought that was my role. I thought this was who I was, the caretaker, so this was what I was supposed to do. "Sacrificial love is the highest form of love" I would hear and read. And that's what I thought I was doing.

Today I know this is called codependency. I didn't realize back then that by playing this role in the relationship, I was also enabling the dynamic to continue. I believed I was being selfless and loving everyone well. I thought I wasn't loved unless I was needed, and they all needed me so much. Love, to me, meant choosing them over me regularly, as in, all the time. This only deepened my codependent tendencies from childhood and ingrained in me the habit of abandoning myself for the sake of love and acceptance from others. It also ensured I never received the connection I so deeply longed for, that I felt resentful and exhausted, always feeling abandoned and alone. Most of all, I was completely disconnected from myself, my body, my feelings, my needs, my wants, my dreams, and my desires. I functioned completely other-focused. And so I thought it was my job to shelter and save the children from seeing their dad drunk. I thought it was my job to help Jim find a way out of the addiction he was under and support him when he couldn't. So I poured myself into others instead of having to face the conflict and pain within myself. Again, like with immigration, I chose to keep busy in order not to face it. And there was a lot to juggle at the time so I continued running forward at high speed without looking back or inward. I silenced my heart when it broke over and over, and stayed on the roller coaster of my life and just did more things, faster, and worked harder. I continued to improve myself as a business owner, to grow as the COO, to expand as an entrepreneur, to challenge myself as a woman, and to stretch myself as a mother and wife. I guess both of us were simply using the coping mechanisms of choice to run from our own trauma. For Jim it was his drinking. For me it was staying busy, chasing, achieving, and pushing myself. Inside, however, we both felt utterly alone and were simply running from our old pain. We just didn't know it. And we wouldn't for a long time, because it worked on the outside. Our business was booming.

It was hard to explain the challenges of running a company that was growing so fast and the stresses that came with it. No one I knew could relate and advise me. It was hard to talk about the delicate balance (or lack of it) of running a business while also having a family life. It was impossible to even bring up the topic of Jim being an alcoholic because people wouldn't believe me. He was always so fun and so nice. For years I tried everything: being angry, being mad, being stern, threatening to leave, promising we'd beat it together, being silent, accepting the disease, being compassionate and helpful, demanding AA and rehab, helping too much or leaving it all to himself to sort out. Nothing worked. Nothing I did worked. The hardest thing was that I just wanted my Jim back. He was still in there and I could see him sometimes, but often it was like he was taken over by a monster. I don't mean to imply he ever hit or hurt us physically. He didn't. But his presence felt unsafe and scary. It was a lonely time. I felt that I made a commitment to be there for my husband—for richer and poorer, through sickness and health—and I was there for Jim through the ups and downs. However, I felt that I did not have the same level of partnership and support back in return. Some days, I could explain it and get through to him and he would get it and he would understand my loneliness and despair, he would see me in my pain. He would cry and promise to get better or to quit. My heart broke for him. Other times, it was as if he wasn't really there, like he was lost inside somewhere and I could not reach him, like he was asleep and I was desperately trying to shake him awake. It was exhausting navigating this space because I just didn't know which Jim I would encounter on any given day. There was so much love but also so much pain simultaneously. It was living prepared for the worst but hoping for the best, a time filled with struggles, disappointment, tension, and too many expectations. It wasn't all bad, of course. There were plenty of good times, fun, family, and tender moments too. He was a wonderful dad and a great husband when he wasn't clouded by the booze. He was tender, silly, gentle, patient, generous, kind, and so loving, but then I would lose him. We would all lose him. He would show up sometimes, for short periods, and be present and engaging, but then he would leave us all, walking toward the basement, down the stairs and into the bar "to work." I compartmentalized it all, managed the crisis and organized the mess, filled my heart with tender love from my kids, celebrated our successes out loud, and often cried alone in the shower or into my pillow at night for no one to see. That's how I survived.

While I had a couple of girlfriends whom I could confide in about parts of my life, I felt like nobody really saw me—all of me—because it wasn't safe to come to anyone as my true, entire self. I was just too much. So I showed up one way for my parents, another way for employees, yet another way for social engagements or business meetings with corporate partners. This felt like wearing the masks, a different one for each segment of the people of my life. I created these divisions so that it would be easier to just keep away the things I didn't want to deal with but come as my "best self" in whichever capacity I was needed. This splitting off into parts meant I always felt alone and unseen, because I wasn't coming anywhere whole and integrated. I wasn't letting myself actually be seen. I felt like I needed to project different images, different versions of myself, to the outside world. For example, as a leader, I always had to be strong. I always had to have my shit together. As a mom, I needed to create safety, peace, and love in our home. As a daughter to my parents, I needed them to know that everything was just fine so that they wouldn't worry (because then I would have to manage that too). In social situations I was the fun, easygoing, energetic one who told great stories and made everyone laugh. Really, everywhere I went I just shared a very small piece of myself. All of these pieces were a part of me, but there wasn't ever a place where I was fully myself. Of course nobody knew I wasn't born in America or the story of fleeing my home for safety or my traumatic immigration years. Nobody. I was always hiding, hiding in plain sight. This was exhausting. I would pay the price for it much later when the outer shell simply couldn't withhold the pressure from within, when the burnout came, and the volcano exploded from the pain of the past I was repressing. But at the time I was simply resigned to the fact that this was my life, sometimes incredibly wonderful and sometimes horrible. I just couldn't deal at all with the horribleness when it came because it would trigger what I had been pushing down since being a small child. I was not allowing any of that to come up. And while I was protecting my heart from feeling the pain of any of my childhood trauma, I closed it off to the world just a bit. When you close your heart, you don't just keep out the bad. You also keep out the good: the love and the joy. This was why sometimes when things were amazing, I felt like I wasn't feeling or receiving it fully. But I needed to do this for survival and so I am thankful I did, despite the fact that it actually caused more pain to build up which I would have to deal with later.

———————————

When AJ was about six months and Mira five and a half years old, I finally broke down and brought in someone to help me. By that time, I had also stopped cleaning the house and got over the guilt of having to pay for a cleaning lady to do my "womanly duties." Seriously, I thought like that! But thankfully the exhaustion and wanting to have a clean house won. I still cooked on weekends and made dinners when I could after work but takeout and pre-prepared meals became more acceptable simply due to lack of time. Nonetheless, I felt guilty about it. Rikki, our babysitter, joined our family at the peak of the company's growth and probably the most chaotic time for our foursome. She helped me by taking Mira to and from activities after school and staying with AJ during the day so I could work in the office. I sent Mira off to school each morning after making her lunch and was home when the school bus dropped her off each day, when I wasn't traveling. No matter what, my work days took a break between 4 p.m. and the kids' bedtime. I was mom full-time then. Rikki became my partner and often my support, when Jim just couldn't show up in that capacity. There was a silent understanding between us, maybe even among the three of us, that she was there for me to lean on. I was thankful for her love for both the children and we took her everywhere we went—and we traveled quite a bit with the business, bringing the kids along. Rikki was always there. I was thankful to be able to open up to her at least a little bit about how hard it all was—she had witnessed enough incidents to know about Jim's addiction and she became my safe person during that time. I felt that we protected the kids together. She loved them too. As did Jim, he was just possessed by this demon he couldn't yet fight off. I did not understand back then that he couldn't get healthy until it was his time, until he himself was ready. That's just how it works. An alcoholic will not get sober for you or for his children. I didn't know and so I just thought he didn't love us enough. No matter how much and how deeply I loved him, he didn't love me enough to quit. I believed that I just wasn't enough ...

———————————

While all of this was part of my reality, there was also a lot of happiness, joy, and excitement at the same time. Jim and I would spend many hours dreaming up new concepts, new ideas, and new visions for our company and our life together. We were always talking about living in the islands, or Europe, or some exciting place we would stumble into while on the road. We envisioned ourselves spending a year in the Caribbean as a family and writing about it—a blog perhaps, or a book, or just content for our website. We sat on flights and drafted and revised itineraries down to how many days we'd spend in each destination and at what time of the year. And then it usually came down to the fact that the kids had it pretty good where we were and stability was probably an important thing for them: safe town, good schools, beautiful and comfortable home, great friends and neighbors. But dreaming up these things was one of our favorite activities. I also loved working with Jim because we made a great team creatively. We were constantly planning, dreaming, and then jumping in headfirst without asking for anyone's permission on the business side of things. It really was a wild ride—building our future together just as we envisioned it—no task was too big. Together, we were fearless. Nothing was impossible. We were always talking about the company and what to improve and how to grow it and what to do better and what crazy thing to take on next. Soon enough we had a billboard in Times Square, a car in the Indy500 race, a TV commercial, a regular radio show, and our own video production team creating content in the islands (before everyone else was doing it). Jim dreamed big and inspired others with his vision and drive. I broke down his aspirations into projects that were actually doable and some that we'd just need to table for later, and created concrete plans for action, execution, and implementation. Jim's way of thinking was "the sky's the limit," and I pulled him down from up there by the ankles and brought him down to the earthly level. He envisioned and painted the big picture and I broke it down, planned, and found ways to make it happen. We made a really good team. He was the visionary and I was his anchor who got shit done.

Everything in life moved so extremely fast. I did not see it back then because I was right in the middle of it but people often asked me how I managed all of it. I did not think it was a big deal because it came naturally and I just didn't know any other way—this was my "normal" life. I moved with lightning speed. But I often wonder this myself now, ten years later. How? It was borderline insane what we did, how fast we did it, and that we came out of it all together still as a married couple and still as a family. It was tense at times, stressful always, scary occasionally, but it drove us both. We lived in a constant state of an adrenaline rush and chaos. And the truth was that I just loved it. It was exciting. It took my gift for working under pressure (perfected in my TV career), love for travel, and drive to lead and succeed and it combined it all into a job that I loved. What prepared me for management the most, however, was being a mom—I spent most of my time sorting out issues that people brought to my office. My job was to listen well, and then to fix it. There was always a lot of drama, whether with the employees in the call center or customers in destinations. People were getting stuck at airports, missing flights, forgetting passports, getting denied boarding, getting drunk and doing dumb things, arriving at hotels and being told they had no booking, arriving at hotels and being told they were getting moved to another hotel because this one was full. Transfer buses would not show up, excursions would forget to pick them up, rooms would not be what was represented in photos, there would be bugs, broken AC, cheap gross alcohol, lost luggage, hurricanes, rain, heat strokes, injuries, hospital visits, helicopter airlifts out due to health issues ... you name it. There was never a dull moment. Things in the Caribbean worked much differently than in the USA, basically *much slower*. So getting anything fixed quickly was often impossible. The Caribbean laid-back vibe is perfect—unless you need to get something done. I could probably write a whole book of its own filled with the crazy and funny (and some sad) stories of what would happen on people's vacations that we had to help them get out of. I always said I was Mom first and COO second. But I loved both my roles and the large family it created. Looking back, I can see that the little girl in me was just trying to rebuild what she left behind in Poland. I was always longing for the family I was torn away from. And CheapCaribbean was just one way I subconsciously tried to bring that back into my life. I had this romanticized vision of our company: my extended relatives whom I treasured. Of course, with it came so much betrayal because I expected everyone who worked for me to "get it," to understand how important they were to me and how much I cared. And I wanted them to not just see it but also to feel the same way in return. I was still trying to fill that deep, empty hole inside of me, to reconstruct a "belonging" in my own way. Creative, perhaps. But, sadly, impossible.

Mamuś and Papuś remained a very important part of our lives. They sold the Baldwin house that we all built together to join us on our new family adventure, both in Pennsylvania as well as in the

Caribbean. They too came to work for the company and bought a new house just ten minutes away from ours. Oftentimes when Jim and I traveled and couldn't bring the kids, my parents would stay home with them. Even more often, they came along with us as we shared with them our passion for the islands and everything we were discovering and building there.

Five years after we started the business, we had an offer on the table for a full buyout in exchange for a large sum of money. The celebration was *huge* but short-lived as very early during the due diligence process, we learned that our accounting was a total and complete disaster. Rather than making millions, we were quite heavily in debt and would run out of money in about ninety days. The news was shocking and devastating. Our amazing and incredible life very quickly started to crumble. The dream we were living became a complete nightmare basically overnight. We were not prepared for it in any way.

We were forced to close several of the offices outside of the main Pennsylvania reservation center. We canceled plans to open up a call center in the UK and expand into Europe. We had to lay off many employees and cut salaries of those who were left. Jim and I took no pay for the next few months and delayed paying all our bills where possible. It was survival time. We needed investors to ensure we stayed alive and people's lives weren't disrupted and ruined by unemployment and layoffs (including of course our own). They're called "angel investors" for a reason and ours swooped in by a miraculous string of events coming together to save CheapCaribbean from a death that seemed inevitable. We had many conversations during this time about the worst-case scenarios: loss of it all, bankruptcy, homelessness, legal issues, possibly jail time, moving in with my parents, what to tell the kids, how to break the news to our team … It was all so awful. There were tears, sleepless nights, stressful phone calls, tense meetings, pure panic sometimes, endless poring over the bills and expenses, and being creative in how to manage it all.

I walked into the basement late one night and found Jim slumped over spreadsheets on his laptop, printouts of numbers, and a glass of Mount Gay Rum and Diet Coke on the side. "Come to bed," I whispered. "Try to get some sleep." He looked up at me with tears in his eyes, and all I could see was the little boy inside of him terrified. Immediately tears rolled down my face and my heart broke into pieces inside me. I walked over to him and held him, both of us crying and shaking. *How did it come to this? What will we do?* I wondered. But what I said was: "I love you. It's going to be okay. Somehow it's gonna be okay. We'll figure it out." Because I trusted that there was a way. There always was, even if we couldn't yet see it.

Also present besides the fear was the instinct and drive to survive, to stay alive, to stay afloat. We didn't come this far not to make it. So we spent many hours every day in closed-door low-voice conversations with our new CFO (who discovered the problem) coming up with plans and strategies to keep things going. The familiar cycle of having to live with trauma as my constant companion was repeating itself yet again. Another crisis to deal with and lead myself through. *Fuck.* But for this, I didn't need to pinch myself to believe it. This feeling and vibe were familiar. It was almost like I was expecting it—things had just gotten *too* good. I got careless and started to believe in "happily ever after."

It was the most stressful and painful time of our lives. Mira was nine and AJ was four. We scraped together any savings we had, sold anything we could get money for (with the exception of our house, which was on mortgage), and maxed out the credit cards trying to save our "third baby"—everything in the company's name was in our name. Losing CheapCaribbean would mean losing it all. In November 2007, on Jim's forty-second birthday, we finally closed the deal. We sold 51 percent of the company we had started just seven years prior in order to avoid bankruptcy. I was thirty-three years old. Life was bringing me to another threshold. I didn't know it but there was a huge shift coming ahead after surviving this storm.

The sale meant that several changes had to take place in how the company was run, and who ran it. We were now minority owners and I was the only woman on our board and one of only two women on our executive team. The Dallas boardroom was a man's world. It was a corporate game with lots of rules, bylaws, legal documents, and processes. There was all of a sudden all this strategic planning, getting approval, checking with the legal team, lots of paperwork, voting on things, Human Resource conference calls, and getting comps on how others do things. It was totally asking us to play within rules—not just of travel, but also corporate laws and regulations. This tied our hands and put us under the control of someone else. It also crushed our creativity and passion for what we were trying to do. Neither of us liked it and neither of us worked well in that environment—it's why we started our own business—to do it how we wanted it done. The fun, exciting days of dreaming up big things and finding ways of making them happen were over. But we had no choice—we needed to do what had to be done in order to save the company and not shatter the lives of the people who worked for and with us, and to save our own butts too!

Gone were the generous maternity program, the good health insurance, the FAM trips, the vacation benefits, the Christmas parties, the fun events, the time off allowed, the customer loyalty program, the benefits of booking with us for our clients (like the Sunshine Guarantee, one of my favorites!). All the things that I was proud of offering to our people and our customers were getting cut back. It was a catch 22. Of course, I was thankful that we got a second chance at life and an opportunity to keep going and continue providing jobs for so many (at our height it was nearly 500 people) and affordable vacations to many more. But I was the one who sat in the main call center with the majority of our staff and had to deliver the bad news to the people I had myself hired—explain it, justify it, and pretend like I agreed with it. I was the one who had to demote close friends, cut their incomes by half, and even fire my own parents (imagine that one!). It sucked. People would ask for meetings in my office to discuss, to question, to resign, to get angry, or to cry. It was getting harder and harder to keep supporting the direction the company was taking, understanding its necessity but also seeing that this was not my vision for CheapCaribbean. It simply became "strictly a business" focused solely on the bottom line, which is what was deemed needed for survival. Jim and I ran it as an extension of our family, which I think now is impossible. I am not sure that you can make financially sound decisions as a business owner and be kind, loving, and generous to your employees. At some point there comes a conflict and you have to make an ugly choice. A nice guy has to get fired because that saves the company money, perhaps to be replaced by someone younger and cheaper. There's no forgiveness in running a big profitable business. No grace. There's just revenue lost and "trimming the fat." These were the new rules that our investors came with. It's what it took to bring us back from the dead. I started to wonder if there was space for me in a business world based on those principles. Tough decisions had to be made for the benefit of the whole, but many of those who worked for us just didn't see it that way. They just saw things getting taken away and did not understand the reasons. And I understood both sides. Eventually I stepped down from my role of running operations. Not only because I could not support the direction the organization was going, but because suddenly I found myself being asked to order lunches for meetings I wasn't invited to or to arrange travel and vacation plans for our new board members. I was stunned. What the fuck was this?!

I felt like some of our new business partners thought I just brought Jim his coffee and kept his calendar all this time. A few saw my value but the majority simply overlooked me and turned to my husband instead. And I had a choice in that moment. I could be the chameleon again and mold myself into what they wanted to see in a leader, a woman in her pantsuit being a total bitch hanging out with the boys, smoking cigars and drinking whiskey, making fun of the foreigners we employed in Poland and Vancouver (imitating their heavy accents in board meetings to erupting laughter). I did that thing I learned to do early on where I took a good look at the situation from high up above and saw the big picture. I assessed my battlefield and quickly figured out what it would take to prove myself to these guys, and I knew I could do it. But I was tired. I was so darn tired of it all, of life and its speed. And my heart was no longer in it. Finally, for the first time I didn't just bend and twist myself into a freaking pretzel for approval and a place in the C-suite. Instead, I said "fuck this" and I thought to myself *No.*

And *no* was a new word for me. I was raised into the world of women always saying yes, even when there was no gas left in the tank and we were barely breathing. "Yes, of course" and "Yes, honey" and "Right away, sir." There was always a way to say yes, and a good girl and a good woman always said yes with a smile. I said so many yeses without realizing that many of those were actually pretty hard noes to myself. And so instead I did this crazy new thing. I sat back and I just witnessed what happened next and I saw myself getting shoved into the back row and eventually out of my own company and into the small office in my home. I didn't fight it, because I suddenly realized that I no longer wanted to play by these fucked-up rules. I no longer wanted to participate in this game. I wanted to lead not by spreadsheets, numbers, projections, and EBITDA—I wanted to lead from my heart, from generosity, from collaboration, and with a team united because we were doing something amazing together, which helped the less fortunate with its profits. I wanted to lead from an overflow of love inside me fueled by a purpose and deeper meaning. And crazy fun! None of that is possible when you're trying to squeeze every dollar out of every booking. It suffocates the soul and the creative flow of people. I was done and I knew it instantly. I knew it in my body, my gut, and in my bones. And of course I knew it in my heart.

I gave up my office in the call center to work from home. As I packed my things into a brown cardboard box and cleared my desk, I thought back to the days of making the front walls of my office glass. I wanted people to always see me and for me to look up from my computer and see them. I didn't want to put in a solid wall because I didn't want separation. I wanted to always feel a part of my team. My door was always open so they could always find me accessible and available. I felt tears forming in my eyes and my cheeks got warm but I kept packing, taking the family photos off my desk, those of my kids and those of company outings. I turned to the left and looked at Jim's office, which hadn't been occupied by him in a while since he worked from home almost exclusively. We put a sliding door between the two rooms, which was also always open, so we could yell one to the other over the projects we were working on, to share and give/receive input and excitement. It all seemed to make my throat feel tight as I held back the tears that wanted to flow. I was grieving. I drove home sad and angry. It would be hard to step back into the office space for many, many years.

I accepted a smaller role with the company, while keeping my seat on the board. It felt like I walked off into the sunset and nobody really cared. Suddenly getting a reply to an email was hard, getting a call returned wasn't guaranteed, because I no longer signed the company's paychecks. It was a hard lesson to learn and a tough transition to go through. Again, I felt betrayed by the people I fought so hard for, my own employees. But they never asked to be given that power over me. I played the victim and felt so terribly sorry for myself and all my losses. I felt misunderstood by the new leadership and board members. Again, I felt isolated, left out, and alone—ah, that familiar environment. I realized how much my role at the company defined who I was. I struggled with this loss of identity, and with the decisions made to keep changing how the "third child" of ours would be raised. I wanted to rescue, fix, and save it. I was so angry about what was happening to my company and also to me. I was miserable. But fear drove this misery. I was so attached to my role as founder and COO that I simply did not know what to do without it. I started cooking and baking things like my name was Julia Child—soups, stews, bread, pasta, soufflé, all the French dishes, and the most complicated of recipes. I read all her books and started making everything from scratch in my kitchen, like a mad scientist in her own laboratory. Desperate to keep busy. Desperate to keep running.

One day a FedEx driver rang our doorbell and handed me an envelope. It was a letter notifying me that my contract with CheapCaribbean would not be renewed. The chairman of the board forgot to call me ahead of time so the letter came at the same time as the lame phone call apologizing for the oversight. I said very little and hung up the phone to open up the white cardboard envelope I had to sign for. I was in our garage. I sat down on a box of turquoise CheapCaribbean Fat Towels, which were stored all over our place. There it was—on the letterhead of the company I cocreated, with the very logo I designed—a short, cold, businesslike note in legalese thanking me for my years of service and contribution. At first I froze and felt nothing looking at the characters forming the words that formed the sentences on the

paper in my hand. And then it hit me like a ton of bricks. I covered
my eyes with my palms as if trying to hide myself from someone,
like a small child covering up her ugly tears. They ran down my
cheeks one after another until they simply became waterfalls of the
sadness I was feeling inside. My breathing became erratic and my
shoulders slumped forward and my body folded in half. I sobbed
for an hour, shocked not just by the news but somewhat caught off
guard by the emotions I was experiencing. It was more than the grief
of the news, the shock of the situation, and the relief of it all. I cried
the tears of the last year, and maybe even the past seven. All it took
to get us here. All it took to reach the heights: my full heart, all my
energy, all my dreams, all my strength, all my time— everything
I was. And then I cried for the awful low times: the struggles, the
sacrifices, the stress, all my energy, all my strength, all my time, my
full heart—everything I was. I got served the termination papers
I delivered to many others before me. I was told I wasn't good
enough in black ink on white paper. I was told I brought nothing
of value, that I was no longer needed, that I didn't matter, that I was
disposable, that they would actually be better off without me. My
husband, however, was important and necessary—one of the boys.
The letter didn't say any of this, but this is what it meant to me. I
cried the tears of where I had come from and how hard I worked
to get to this point. I sobbed for the little Marta within me, scared
and wondering what she would do next. I cried for the immigrant
girl inside feeling unseen and deemed unworthy yet again. I cried
for the teenager not fitting in and never belonging, and I cried for
the lost grown woman I suddenly became aware of—the mom, the
wife, the business woman, the entrepreneur—everything in her life
was slowly slipping out of her control. This scared the shit out of
me.

———————

The next couple of years were unsettling and I struggled to find myself and a good balance in life. Work was such a huge part of who I was and I didn't know what to do next. Jim was still employed by CC and was now given financial targets and deadlines to meet in order to make his salary. This produced a lot of stress and pressure at home. I remained a member of the board of directors not because I had a passion for it, not because I wanted to keep in touch, but because I needed a paycheck. It was sad to do that after years of getting paid for doing jobs I enjoyed. Especially the last one, which I felt I birthed somehow. It was a disorienting time and I leaned heavily on my girlfriend Kristen, who always kept me from drowning on the mommy front. There were so many dates and events and tasks in the local schools, kids' activities, and at church, and she just kept me on track. Our daughters were best friends. We quickly became best friends too. She would rescue me when other mommies would look at me funny because the cupcakes I brought to the classroom for parties were from the grocery store and not homemade while I was still working. Or when I didn't know what Portfolio Night meant at the school or was away for a youth group event, or forgot that it was crazy hair day on Friday. We would also carpool the girls to karate, lacrosse, playdates, birthday parties, and church events, which was a lifesaver. We went on long walks with her sheepdog Riddley, after the kids were off to school in the mornings, wondering what next, who I was, and how to move forward from here. Serious talks about life, marriage, and kids, and also very serious discussions about highlighting our hair and cooking or baking the latest dish I was mastering. I am forever grateful to her for holding me through this transition in my life and staying a soul-sister to me to this day.

Once I stopped working, I really poured myself into the kids (besides my time in the kitchen). AJ was in second grade and Mira just starting middle school. Both had very difficult school years, as it turned out, so it felt right for them to have their mom with them full-time. Or that's how I justified it. In reality, I needed them to ground me because I was swimming in the unknown and drowning in it. I needed something as a reference of my place in the world and a reminder of my own identity. My babies reminded me of my most important job—being their mama. This allowed me to breathe and not freak out completely. It caught me midway through my downward spiral into lostness and stabilized me. Rikki was getting married and starting a family of her own so it just seemed like it was meant to be, like it was divine timing for everything. AJ had a very challenging teacher and often came home crying. He hated school. He also just couldn't sit still, through classes, the bus ride, the homework, even dinners at home. Mira struggled with the transition into middle school: getting up at 5:15 in the morning for a 6:15 a.m. yellow-bus pickup (who made *that* crazy schedule?!) and dealing with a much larger school and managing a lot more workload and responsibilities. She was stressed and went through a period of having seizures and even fainted in the shower once while getting ready for school. It was a tough time for us all. I was thankful to be there for them both at what seemed like critical stages of their lives. But then it started to affect my well-being too and I found myself sometimes short with the kids or impatient.

For the first time in my life, I started to become aware of the anxiety so very present in my body, which nobody spoke about back then. I didn't know what it was, but I felt this force and energy rushing inside of my body like a pressure cooker, trying to force its way out. The only thing I could think of doing was trying to keep it in, to make it go away, to contain and control it. It scared me, which only seemed to make everything worse. The experience rattled and shook me to my core.

I was driving home from Jules Pizza early one evening, where

I took the kids as a treat for dinner. It was our favorite thin-crust pizza spot in the area. Mira and AJ sat in the back seat of the car, busy with their devices. Mira was listening to her iPod and AJ was playing a game on his PlayStation Portable. I had driven this route a million times and knew we were less than fifteen minutes from home, the long curvy roads of Bucks County filled with green trees and beautifully landscaped homes. I looked through the windshield of my BMW and I didn't recognize the area before me. *Where the heck are we?!* I asked myself. *How the hell did I just get lost?!* Angry with myself, I pulled over on the side of the road, my heart racing. I looked around and tried to mentally retrace my steps from the restaurant, to the car, to the driving … I had no recollection of the turns I had taken. I was operating completely on autopilot. Realizing this scared me even more. *How did I get here and how the hell is it that I can't remember?!* I thought about driving to the office over and over and it becoming so automatic that I would blink and be there and not remember the drive. *Isn't that dangerous?! How the hell does it even happen that I don't blow through red lights or hit an occasional deer who jumps out at me while I'm behind the wheel?!* Thoughts racing through my head, I still had no idea where we were. *Something must be wrong with my brain, my memory. Maybe it's an early sign of Alzheimer's. Shit.* My breathing started to get shallow and quick and then I was gasping for air. I rolled down my window feeling the cool breeze on my cheeks. I drank it in, inhaling deeply. "You okay, Mama?" asked Mira. She always knew. And I lied to her and said, "Yes, honey. All good. Just need a minute." What could I tell her that wouldn't scare a little girl? Better to keep trying to suppress it all. But it was hard. I input the address of our house into my BlackBerry's GPS to get us home safely. I texted my parents to meet me there because I didn't know what was happening and Jim was away in Dallas. I drove slowly and made it back barely able to breathe, images in front of my eyes appearing fuzzy, and tears streaming down my face. *What the fuck was this?*

The emergency room diagnosis I received that evening was "dehydration," first of several. My parents were concerned, my mom especially worried. Jim was not thrilled to get the call in the middle of his meetings that I needed him to come back and help me. He still traveled often, which made me feel even more alone in our marriage but even more desperately connected to the kids as my source of love and belonging. That's a lot of pressure to put on two little people—I understand that now, but they were my everything and all my days and my feelings were completely controlled by how they reacted to me and how they came home from school (which hadn't been great lately). If they were happy, I was happy. If they were sad, I was sad. I cooked amazing dinners, I did homework with Mira and AJ, I drove them to their activities—I mom'ed really hard. I was determined. It was lonely with Jim away, but in some ways it was even more challenging when Jim was home because, as much as I wanted him around, when he was home routine went out the window; rules went out the window; normalcy went out the window. I let it all go and I called myself "flexible" and proud of being able to "just go with the flow." What I really was doing instead was abandoning myself and letting his addiction-driven chaos take over, because it got too hard to fight him on things and constantly be forced to play the responsible parent (the bad cop) while he did the fun and crazy things. And I didn't want the kids to see any of that. I wanted so badly to protect and shield them. So I'd let things slide, harboring resentment inside because I didn't have the strength to speak up for what I thought was important. I couldn't handle the tension (inside of myself or between the two of us) and I wanted the home to be a place of peace and love, but I hated his temper and one-sided way of seeing things. Deep down inside I also feared it, so I avoided it like the plague. It was just easier to say nothing—and let the kids giggle and laugh, stay up late on a school night, and spend time with their dad. I considered it all a small price to pay for having him around and engaged.

But amid this chaos and tension, a deep energy of love flowed through and among us. I can only call it miraculous and somehow sacred because through it all, it held us together like superglue. No matter how good or how bad things got, we always came back to each other and to love. It was sort of like a divine undercurrent running through and around us. It's what made us survive and stay a family after everything, something not of our own efforts or doing but completely otherworldly. A larger field of love holding us all tenderly. I realized that it was familiar. I knew it from before... The four lonely and lost immigrants in Brooklyn... It was the same love now surrounding my own family.

# CHAPTER 8

# The Perfect Life

## PARIS, FRANCE

### 2012

We arrived in Paris that summer with four suitcases and the intention of spending two months in an apartment we rented on Rue Saint-André des Arts. It was June of 2012, twelve years after the inception of CheapCaribbean.com and twenty-six years after my arrival in America as a political refugee. Jim and I had been together for sixteen years and the kids were fourteen and nine. I stopped working full-time earlier that year, and we enrolled the children in online school (which was rather rare at the time) so that we could travel as a family and not get in trouble with the school board for missing too many days. We visited friends in Mexico where we paddle boarded in the Pacific Ocean and learned about the rare Blue Footed Boobies, birds only found in that part of the world. We took a tour of California visiting Hollywood (for Mira) and Legoland (for AJ), as well as driving down the coastline and stopping at the San Diego Zoo. We spent time with family in Indiana (where Jim is from), attended two family weddings, flew to Canada for Father's Day and back to Pennsylvania for Mother's Day with my parents. We headed over across the Atlantic Ocean and toured London and its attractions, as well as Harry Potter Studios, just outside the city. All of this was also education, the kind missing in the schools Mira and AJ attended and the kind that was important to me as a person of multiple cultures. I wanted my kids to be exposed to different ways of living, thinking, and functioning. In mid-June we boarded the Eurostar train crossing the Chunnel from London to Paris. We had no idea this would turn into six years of living in France, similar to visiting the Caribbean and not knowing it would become our second home for the decade that followed our first trip to St. Martin.

We had been coming to Paris a few years in a row, each summer staying a little longer, so we had gotten to know the city quite well. It was a long-standing love affair with the French capital since Jim proposed to me here fourteen years earlier. This time, we had six weeks to spend revisiting our favorite spots and discovering new ones while staying in the St. Germain district (also known as the 6th arrondissement). The kids were enrolled in a bilingual summer camp to learn the language, experience the culture, and spend time with others their age, while Jim and I explored the City of Light.

Each morning, we took Mira and AJ to the International School of Paris together by metro and then stopped for a French breakfast of croissants and coffee nearby after drop-off. Many times, other parents joined us and we quickly started tapping into a local community of expats, foreigners, and Americans overseas living in Paris. We spent the rest of the day roaming the streets of the French capital. Just the two of us getting lost in the various districts and ending up somewhere new each time for lunch, which was normally a two-hour affair. Some days I brought heels and we'd try a fancy Michelin-rated place recommended by our new friends, but most times we preferred local places, jeans and sneakers, in off-the-beaten-path cafés. I loved learning and practicing my French, because let's face it, everything sounds better in French, even ordering a salad and a glass of wine. We strolled through parks and gardens; wandered around grand boulevards and tiny charming cobblestone streets; stopped into amazing museums, beautiful department stores, and little family-owned shops; checked out markets, art exhibits, and flower fairs. We walked across bridges over the river Seine, or down by its banks, stopping for a baguette sandwich and a half bottle of bubbly for lunch on a nearby bench, always admiring the incredible architecture and history all around us. It was beautiful and as romantic as it sounds. I felt like I was living in a movie and I didn't want it to end.

By this time, I was fully out of the day-to-day operations of CheapCaribbean.com while Jim was still overseeing the marketing, advertising, and product departments. When 3 p.m. Paris-time came around (which was 9 a.m. on the East Coast in the United States), Jim went back to the apartment to work and I headed to pick up the kids from camp. While my weekday mornings were spent with my husband, in the afternoons I was a full-time mom. It was a perfect balance of the two most important roles in my life, once I stopped working, and I loved it. In Paris, it was enough. Here, I felt that I was enough. Mira, AJ, and I rode the metro back "home" making a stop at a local bakery for an afternoon snack. While the kids rested and played after camp, I busied myself with grocery shopping and preparing our family dinners. I loved strolling through our local market, visiting the local farmers and their stands, and picking out fresh ingredients for whatever I would make for dinner that evening. I was still channeling my inner Julia Child and mastering original French recipes, but doing it in France was so much more pleasurable. On weekends I would usually have something simmering or slow-cooking in the kitchen all day filling the whole apartment with delicious smells. I stopped baking in Paris mainly because the desserts in the local bakeries were freshly prepared each day and simply looked like designer artwork and, of course, tasted incredible! Our Saturdays were dedicated to doing something fun as a family and discovering what the city had to offer for families with children. There was plenty! One of our favorite activities was going to Luxembourg Park and spending hours at the kids' playground there; another was hitting the summer fair in the Tuileries Gardens outside the Louvre Museum; or riding bumper cars and jumping on giant outdoor trampolines in the Bois de Boulogne (mainly the kids doing the jumping and me taking pictures and drinking in their laughter). Usually we ended our adventures out at our favorite ice cream shop, Amorino's, where the ice cream is shaped like a rose flower inside the cone (another reason not to make dessert). Sundays were for sleeping in, having brunch at home with fresh, warm pastries from the local bakery, and going to the American Church in Paris. We attended the afternoon contemporary service and afterward spent time mingling with church members, visitors, and tourists over coffee hour, meeting more new friends, while the kids attended youth group. Sunday dinner was always on the walk back "home" to our place—at Tribeca restaurant on rue Cler in the 7th arrondissement.

We got into this routine pretty quickly, and as the planned end to our Paris adventure came nearer, it was clear that we did not want to leave this way of living nor this special place. And just like all the years prior, we started asking "What if we just stayed?!" "What if all this could be our life?" We had a history of threatening not to return from most trips we took, usually planning making living in the Caribbean islands into a reality. We loved envisioning ourselves starting over together in new places—just the four of us and a good Wi-Fi connection—but eventually would end up on a flight back home. This time, however, we finally did it. We held a family meeting over thin-crust pizza at one of our favorite Italian restaurants on Ile St. Louis and decided all together to give Paris a try for one year. A trial run—the Paris experiment. We didn't go home.

I was very aware of the fact that Mira was the same age I had been when we left Poland, and I did not want her experience to be anything like mine. We were already familiar with Paris and it was almost our second home (or third, after the islands!). We weren't going to some strange far-off place with no point of reference. We also had no fears of never being able to return, like when I was a child. Our home back in Pennsylvania was there to go back to if the experiment didn't work out at any point. We even made definite plans to go back for Christmas, so the first part of the long stay was four months. There were no hard and painful goodbyes or secret-keeping about running away—our home was waiting, as well as all our friends. We were also not leaving our country for fear of imprisonment or lack of safety; we weren't running away. We were choosing to stay (versus being forced to flee) in order to experience a different way of living for a while, a way that seemed to fit us all better as a family. This was probably the most important part: there was a choice, we all had a say in it, and we decided together. It was really important to me that the experience not be as shocking and traumatizing as it had been for me. I was very focused on making the kids feel safe, comfortable, and happy. Finding the right place to live (with no cockroaches or drug dealer park in sight) was crucial. Enrolling them in English-speaking schools with resources to help them adapt was my priority. We had the luxury of choice in all of this, unlike my parents. I started to understand how helpless they must have felt watching me struggle and suffer during those early days in America. I was thankful I could do something to ensure that wasn't the way it would go for my babies. I was grateful for this privilege and freedom, which only came to me as a result of the difficult journey of coming to America.

The challenging tasks of finding a furnished place to live on such short notice and international schools with two open spaces required some legwork, research, and serious follow-up. If it meant I could live in Paris, I would find a way! I was the queen of figuring things out and making them happen! The tricky thing about Paris, or much of France really for that matter, is that nothing gets done in the summer. I learned that the whole city shuts down while everyone goes on vacation, especially in July and August. It was a ghost town. Trying to get business done—*c'est ne pas possible!* The difficulty with international schools is that there aren't many, they are all quite small, and they tend to fill quickly. Some even have waiting lists from embassies, governmental agencies, and large corporations who bring people over to Paris on work assignments. Well, it turned out to be possible, after all, if I was willing to not take "*non*" for an answer. I bought us some time and extended the summer apartment rental until the end of August, then focused on schools for Mira and AJ. One thing at a time. That's always how I tackle a massive task, by breaking it into smaller manageable steps. I was off to the races.

We visited three different international schools in Paris and none of them worked. One was too far out in the suburbs and while half of it was brand spanking new, part of it badly needed reconstruction and felt depressing. Bummer. The second, while acceptable, didn't have space for both the kids and could only offer us a waiting list. Not a good sign. The third was split into two cramped campuses, located in the middle of the city, and did not offer sports our kids wanted to play. Well, shit! Things were looking rather gloomy and, discouraged, we headed to the last scheduled visit, at Marymount International School. This final appointment, in Neuilly-Sur-Seine, would determine whether or not we'd get to stay in France. You know, no pressure … The school was warm, small, beautiful, charming, surrounded by a lovely garden and lots of trees, and it felt homey and welcoming. A miracle! Located in the suburbs just outside of Paris, it was reachable by public transportation and offered its own busing system for students. It was a private Catholic school but also a community of many cultures, faiths, and nationalities. Classes were taught in English, there were daily lessons of French, as well as religion/faith/ethics.

It was perfect. We loved the atmosphere, the small campus, and the friendly faces we encountered everywhere. The best news was that they had space for both Mira and AJ to start the upcoming fall, which was only a month away. When the interview and tour ended, we walked out the front gate and paused for a moment. This was it. We let out a collective exhale. Then Jim broke down first. Tears streaming down his face, he held out his arms to the rest of us and we quickly joined him in a huge family hug. All of us were crying! We would get to stay after all! It felt like a sacred moment and divine timing, and it was. It changed the course of our lives—each of our lives individually—and our life together as a family. We became Parisians on that August afternoon, simply with four suitcases of our family belongings. So similar to my early beginnings in Brooklyn (starting over with almost nothing) but at the same time so different.

The only thing left at this point was a rather lengthy application process. And, oh yeah, a permanent place to live after our summer rental expired. The only problem was, we were booked on a cruise to the Mediterranean from a town in the south of the United Kingdom, Southampton. Originally this was going to be the end of our summer vacation and from there we would head to London and return to the United States. Since the cruise wasn't cancelable, we set out for the two-week sail, me just barely finalizing the paperwork to apply to Marymount. While on the cruise, we got the good news that both the kids were accepted, which we celebrated during a stop in Lisbon, Portugal. While in the port of Gibraltar, where the continents of Europe and Africa almost touch, I was frantically faxing applications for apartments from internet cafés. I would find listings online while we had a Wi-Fi connection at sea, in between port stops, scouring the French real-estate listings while learning new words in a new language. We explored the coast of Spain and toured Barcelona where I sent inquiries for more apartments, not hearing back from the others. By the time we reached the South of France and visited Cannes, Monte Carlo, and Nice, I had some solid leads. From Rome (where we saw the Vatican and Sistine Chapel) and Naples (where pizza was invented and also devoured), I negotiated the terms of the lease and, using dial-up, sent back the signed agreement. The cruise ship made a turn there to begin the sail back, and by the time we were touring Palma, the capital of the Spanish island of Mallorca, we had a home to return to in Paris. Perfect timing! Mission accomplished.

Our new apartment was a small two-bedroom with one bathroom and a tiny balcony. It was much, much smaller than our house (and required a toilet schedule) but it had a view of the Eiffel Tower and was in a great residential area of one of the most popular districts in the city (the 7ème arrondissement). AJ was forever telling everyone that we lived in a hotel because he didn't quite get the idea of apartments since he'd only lived in a house in the USA. The place came with all the furniture, kitchen appliances, and everything necessary to live so all we brought were our clothes and personal belongings—our summer luggage. It was surreal going "back to school shopping" in Paris, getting the kids backpacks, pens and pencils, and notebooks. Everything was so different, and somehow so fancy because it was French! The little girl in me was alive and overjoyed! School supplies were my childhood pleasure! Everything was so exciting (at least, to me!). We bought things like a printer and ink and paper (slightly different size than in the USA, we discovered), and for every little thing, we had to learn which store to go to and then drag our shopping back on the metro or bus or in our little grocery trolley while walking back. We did not have a car, similar to those first days of my arrival in the USA, but somehow filled with joy and color this time. It was in a way redoing what I did when I arrived in America but in a completely different way. It felt like a gift. It was deeply healing for me to be able to have choice and to decide, for myself, and then to discuss and give my children choice and a voice in what was going to happen. We chose to stay. We chose where to live. I could now afford the pretty notebooks and the backpacks they wanted. I could say yes, where my parents had to say no. I wanted so badly for Mira and AJ to love it, to make friends, and to be happy. I wanted to give them what I didn't have myself, which was, I realized, exactly what my parents did by bringing Ania and me to America. They gave my sister and me what they did not have as children. And as parents, that's the best we can offer, a better life (plus an extra-large helping of love!).

That fall Mira and AJ started Marymount International School, eighth grade for our daughter and third grade for our son. For the first two weeks, I was pinching myself and squealing with excitement as the kids left on their fancy new school bus from the front steps of the beautiful church that housed Napoleon's Tomb, complete with a view of the Eiffel Tower. *This must be the most picturesque school bus in all of the world!* I was convinced. The first morning they drove off in the big white Mercedes Benz school shuttle, Jim and I both cried. We held each other, watched them go, and we cried. We simply couldn't believe that *we get to do this*! I couldn't believe this was my life. I put all my efforts into making our new apartment feel like a home for our family and getting to know our new neighborhood. Jim and I started locating our favorite bakeries, cheese shops, butchers, flower shops, wine stores, pharmacies, and getting to know the local merchants. It's all part of the French way of doing life, establishing rapport and building relationships. Once your florist recognized you as a "regular" and gave you a deal on your flowers, you knew you had officially arrived. It took me six years at *le fleuriste*! Jim, however, was beloved at our local *boulangerie* by all the older French ladies immediately—he spoke five words of French and charmed everyone into getting the best hot baguettes each time.

Starting over as a family in France wasn't easy, however. It is so difficult in fact, that books, articles, and blogs are written about it and for a while I wrote a family blog for our friends and family, as well as a column for a magazine sharing my experience. I called it "WTF: Welcome To France," which was a term of endearment the expatriate community would utter when encountering super "French" things that made no sense but were unavoidable. For example, when you needed to have an account in a French bank in order to lease a long-term apartment *but* you needed to have an apartment/residential address in order to open up an account in a French bank. You'd just throw your hands up and say "WTF! Welcome To France!" Or when you learned that you needed to go to the pharmacy to buy baking soda, that brown sugar did not exist in France (this has since changed!), and that the post office was funny about delivering packages. Sometimes they came, sometimes not, other times you had to pay duty tax on the content of the parcel. I learned that the hard way when I asked a girlfriend to ship me my favorite rain boots, only to pay $120 for the comfort of having them, once they arrived after being missing for weeks. We got clever and invited a couple we loved dearly to come visit us for Thanksgiving, asking them to please bring some of our fall clothes and jackets, because all we had with us were summer things. Paying for their airline tickets was a lot less expensive than replacing everything, plus we had guaranteed guests for Turkey Day complete with American cranberry sauce and stuffing, both of which also did not exist in France at the time. Some things I was willing to make from scratch but other "delicacies" traditionally needed to come from a box or a can for this holiday! Ordering a turkey was a whole other adventure, as a matter of fact. You had to do it at the butcher weeks in advance. What we also learned, also the hard way, was that you also had to specify that you wanted it baked. The small Parisian apartment ovens would not fit a bird large enough for our American feast. Imagine our surprise when one year Jim showed up at the butcher with a friend to pick up the turkey we ordered for our two families only to find it raw. All our side dishes were hot and ready and we were starving and eager to dig in. The butcher handed the guys a raw turkey, and once he realized there was a misunderstanding, he offered to "quickly" bake it for them. The guys spent two hours waiting in a local brasserie having beers. My friend and I drank a whole bottle of champagne, ate an entire wheel of truffle brie cheese, reheated everything again and again, and played games with our kids. At last we had a baked turkey! Another year a different girlfriend made the mistake of saying "oui" when the butcher asked if she wanted the turkey stuffed. It cost her nearly $150 extra for the bird because the stuffing was apparently a fancy version of foie gras (French delicacy of duck liver), which the butcher did not disclose at the time. You know, you live and you learn. Or as the French say, *c'est la vie!*

Even though navigating life in France was often challenging (relearning how to do the simplest of things that came as second nature to us "back home" in a foreign culture, language, and town), life here was simply beautiful. The pace of things slowed down significantly and we all learned what the French called the *joie de vivre* (joy of living), which is just enjoying the small things in life by simply being present. It was taking the two- (sometimes three-) hour-long lunches. It was having the dessert. It was eating all the carbs in the form of warm baguettes and fresh croissants. It was going to the florist to buy the beautiful fresh bouquets just to have them at home. "Are these a gift or for the house?" the florist would ask and still wrap them up beautifully when I'd answer "They are for me." It was admiring the storefront windows and their magnificent displays—from tiny chocolates to grand designer clothes—everything was an art form to be absorbed and appreciated. It was walking slower and really taking the time to enjoy the beauty of the city, in the sunlight and in the rain. And it was also vacationing right: a cycle of six weeks of school and two weeks off for ten months, followed by the long summer holiday. All the exploring—this was my dream come true! We discovered skiing in the French Alps and "always" went to a little ski town called Chamonix over ski break. We spent All Saints Break in Poland with my family praying over the graves of loved ones gone with living relatives (as local tradition has it). We celebrated Mira's birthday at Lake Como or in Venice in Italy. We spent Easter visiting friends in Slovenia and Germany. We took long weekends in London, Brussels, Spain, or the South of France. Adding to all the travels over the holidays was the fact that both the kids played sports, and when our little international school went to play games "on the road," it meant going to Helsinki, Belgium, The Hague, Frankfurt, Zurich to name a few. Mira even traveled to Rome one year with the school choir for a competition. What a life!

Each year the school also held what was called the May trip, and for one week each grade went somewhere different in France to learn about that particular region of the country. No parents—not even as chaperones. I was a nervous wreck the whole time the kids were away. No cell phones were allowed and no calling home was permitted unless it was an emergency. It was a good exercise for the whole family, and I learned from other mommies who had done this before me to trust that the kids would be okay, slowly letting them go (while they probably breathed a sigh of relief!). We would reunite at the Paris train station on Friday evenings, nervous and excited about how our babies did. They always came back with lots of fun stories, exhausted from the lack of sleep and spending so much time outside. One year, AJ confessed, he didn't brush his teeth the whole time he was away. Both he and Mira treasured these adventures. Especially the eighth-grade trip where they visited Stratford Upon Avon in England where William Shakespeare was born. They got to experience how a play is put on, from makeup to props to rehearsals and the night of the show. Beats the hell out of reciting "to be or not to be" while seated in a boring old classroom! What an incredible way to learn. Our first year in Paris was like a honeymoon, but for the whole family. The kids were thriving in their school, learning the language, getting comfortable, making new friends, and I just loved the international and worldly education they were getting and the life experience of sharing their everyday with various cultures and nationalities of their classmates. I felt like I was helping to raise good "world citizens" and honoring my European roots while paying tribute to the American culture also within our family. I really appreciated the independence living in a city was teaching the kids. Gone were the days of arranging and driving to/from playdates in various homes. Things here just didn't function that way. With no family car and plenty of public transportation (and later Uber), the kids got to learn how to navigate some things themselves. They also spent a lot of their time exploring the city on their own with friends—Paris as their playground—which was scary at first. It was again a great lesson for us all in our own independence, and I found myself with space and time to have a life of my own outside my family or work. It seemed to have been something I had forgotten or somehow lost along the way. Adopted by our new tribe at Marymount International School and the American Church in Paris, I was surrounded by women of all ages, races, nationalities, cultures, and economic backgrounds coming to Paris for various things: jobs, education, love, freedom, adventure, safety, family, fun, a new beginning—or just like us, they came, they fell in love with Paris, and they stayed. I treasured their stories and getting to know them. They made me feel like our decision to stay wasn't weird or crazy—I was normal here. My soul felt at home. Like perhaps this life was the result of that magnetic pull I had been experiencing during my European summers in college in the States. Living here in France, among other foreigners (including Americans), just felt right.

I always considered myself an outsider. I wasn't really Polish because I left my home country at twelve. I wasn't really American either. Neither culture felt like my own. Of course, I wasn't French at all, but what I had stumbled into here was a whole community of outsiders just like me. I found myself among people from all over the world struggling with the same issues—being the (resident) alien. Our church, for example, was made up of over forty different nationalities, all strangers in a new land. The Marymount community was a multifaith, multicultural group as well. Not belonging to France, we all somehow belonged to each other, which made the bonds between us only much stronger. Because being the unwelcomed stranger is hard and painful. We clung to each other and leaned on one another to figure things out, to figure life out. I started to realize how much of my time was spent observing my environment and the people in it and imitating them. Here, everyone was so diverse and so different, at first I was confused. *How do we play this game? What are the rules? Whose lead do I follow and who do I become like in order to be accepted?* That was my formula for survival, and quickly I realized it wouldn't work here. Something else was at play. And that wonderful something felt like home to me even though I couldn't quite put my finger on what it was. This group of non-belongers and exiles, all proud of their roots and heritage, somehow wove together this magnificent blanket of a large, diverse, and beautiful family. I started to wonder what it might be like if I didn't have to become like everyone around me but instead brought my own color of threads, fabrics, and ribbons to this tapestry we were all somehow cocreating? But who exactly was that? Who was I if I wasn't becoming like those around me and trying to do it better? Compare, compete, and conquer—that's what I normally did to fit in. I needed a new strategy but I wasn't sure what it was just yet. In the beginning I was just fascinated by the wide range of opinions, customs, cultures, beliefs, ways of thinking, and the rich stories of the lives these people had lived. What was also touching to me was the radical welcome this community brought forth. It was like each of us had known so well what it was like to be unwelcomed and unwanted, what it was like to be the lonely unloved newcomer, that we went overboard making those new in Paris feel seen, loved, included, and supported. For the first time in my adult life, I started sharing that I came from Poland—reluctantly at first—without shame or steeling myself for a strange reaction. Slowly and little by little, I began retelling the immigration story and welcoming back those rejected and hidden parts of my life and of myself. I started to get vulnerable and honest and truly show myself, from the inside. I began sharing my heart and even some of the deepest pain that had been hidden in there for so long. I allowed my guard to come down and it felt scary, risky, unfamiliar, uncomfortable, and so very messy. I came to see and recognize the façade, the front, that I always hid behind: the busy, successful, professional, hard-working mom and businesswoman who had it all covered and didn't need help. It had kept me safe and distanced enough not to get hurt by others, but it also prevented all the good things from entering in. I had kept most friendships just surface-based acquaintances, preventing anyone from getting too close and truly seeing the real me, the depths of who I was. I didn't know how to share that part of myself—I couldn't put it into words—I didn't even know her myself. I had built a wall around me, around my heart, armor I would wear for protection, which started to get really heavy and also prevented me from ever reaching that thing that I had been so deeply longing for since we left Poland, a true connection and honest belonging. The safety came at a price. It guaranteed that my deepest needs and desires (of finally not being the outsider) stayed just out of reach because I was completely unapproachable.

I didn't know at the time that this was how I had been living since I was twelve. The protective layer slowly started to gently soften as I began to recognize and appreciate that what I loved about the friends I was making here was the uniqueness they each brought and the pain and suffering they were so openly sharing. Their struggles mirrored mine. Their stories echoed mine. It was beautiful. Pretty soon I was making coffee dates and volunteering where I could at the church and at the kids' school to spend time with this new family who had welcomed us in.

Jim was also feeling this love and belonging in our new community. He was very involved at the church, played drums in the contemporary worship band, hosted an expat radio show and a podcast on American sports from Paris. He coached basketball at the kids' school and emceed several fundraiser events, and when not traveling to away games, he was flying back to the States or the Caribbean for work. Coach Jim was everyone's favorite because he was so positive and encouraging and always smiling. I loved watching him play with his teams (especially our own little basketball players). Jim was a kid at heart (still is today!) and just brought joy everywhere. It was in Paris that he shed the nickname of "Caribbean Jim" to become "Joyful Jim." Things were changing for us yet again.

That fall Marymount held something called International Day. It was a special event where all the nationalities attending the school gathered together by country and each organized a table showcasing their culture. There were plenty of moms at the American table so something nudged me to sign up for running the Polish table. I was the only one. I learned that a long-time friend of Papuś (they were buddies since childhood) was living right outside of Paris. I asked him if he would join me in hosting the Polish table during International Day. He just happened to have two traditional Polish outfits, one for a man and one for a woman. I made Polish sweets, he brought some food he prepared himself, and we decorated our station in white and red and stole the show! I surprised myself by how naturally this choice came to me and I also surprised my parents. But it just felt right. So while I loved hosting the Polish table, I also loved celebrating American Thanksgiving in France. This was the kind of life I wanted. This felt good to me.

At Christmas time we traveled back to the United States to visit friends and family for the holidays (and also to restock on all our favorite things at Target). It was so heart-warming to watch the kids take such joy in doing little things they missed. Getting their favorite sandwich at Wawa, eating American cereal for breakfast, ordering American-Chinese takeout, and having endless sleepovers with their best pals. Time also came to reassess our Paris experiment and most likely discuss returning back to the United States. We couldn't afford to stay longer while keeping our home in Pennsylvania. We sat as a family again and held the second ever family meeting, this one in the living room of our Bucks County home, which was decorated for Christmas. We made the hard decision that it was time to come back, even though it made us all sad. Selling our home seemed too scary and traumatic for the kids and it was what we would need to do to be able to keep living in Paris. Mira and AJ were not ready for that step, and we honored their feelings and began moving forward with school applications back in Pennsylvania the following year. Wanting to live my dream life in Paris was one thing. Doing it at the cost of traumatizing my kids was another. I could deal with my sadness and disappointment if it meant not breaking their little hearts.

We flew back to Paris, determined to make the most of the months left before the summer, and we did. Then, just before it was time to start packing and saying goodbye, a magical thing happened. After thirteen years of raising our "third child," CheapCaribbean.

com, an unexpected offer came in for the purchase of our business. The company was bought for enough money to alleviate our financial burdens, and the biggest gift of this was the indefinite extension of the Parisian life.

We closed the sale of CheapCaribbean while in the USA on summer vacation at the end of year one. We celebrated this with lots of champagne. Ah … I'd get to live in the land of our favorite sparkling beverage—forever! We flew back to Paris and celebrated again, moving into a larger apartment and renting it as full-time, long-term residents. It became official and based on my Polish passport, the whole family could legally stay, since France is part of the European Union. We began to make the place our own, purchasing furniture, plates and glasses, pots and pans, towels and trash cans, curtains and wall paintings. Really starting over. I hired an interior decorator and she helped me find sheets and carpets, bedding and pillows, appliances and silverware, lamps and side tables. She ordered our beds and took me shopping for couches. She remodeled old bathrooms and decorated the kids' rooms. It became my most beloved home and I loved every minute of this process, just like building our house in Jamison, Pennsylvania. Just like pinching myself while the framing of our custom home was going up in Bucks County, I was pinching myself while furnishing my Parisian place. It was a beautiful three-story townhouse in the middle of a private, quiet courtyard with its own garden and patio space—an unheard-of find in the city of tiny apartments. I put utilities in our name, ordered our own internet service and phone line, met the concierge of our building and started learning who our new neighbors were. It was incredible. It was already amazing the year prior but the dream life just got even better. We had money in the bank, we didn't need to work for a while, *and* we were in Paris to stay!

It was amazing how little we brought back with us from

America. What was even more amazing was how much of the stuff that filled our large home there we could live without. Life got so much simpler and it just worked for us. We figured if we could live without it for a year, we could live without it. So we just brought a few sentimental things and our favorites and left everything else behind. There wasn't a "move." With the money from the sale of the company, we paid off our house in the USA and rented our townhouse in France. This felt safe to the kids—home was always waiting, a security blanket. And so year two began, and surely it was going to be even more amazing than year one!

It truly was the perfect life for me and for the first time since Poland, I let myself grow roots. I wasn't looking to go away all the time with my suitcase partially packed, just in case. I didn't need to escape to the Caribbean and run away to Europe in order to feel okay. Where I was living finally and at last became enough. It became home. And the community we found became the family I had been searching for since leaving Szczecin. I felt that I belonged; that I had found my people. I felt that I was loved. So I stopped looking for more. I stopped running. I finally felt safe. I settled down. I had everything I could ever want. This was it. To commemorate the sale of the company, we decided to go to St. Barths on a family vacation.

And this is where it all broke. The perfect exterior façade; the life I tried so hard to craft, curate, and arrange so carefully and with so much effort; my hard-earned success … It all crumbled.

I had everything I could ever want. I was living my dream life. What exactly was the problem? When I thought my life was over, that night in St. Barths and all the weeks that followed, I couldn't understand what was happening to me or why. All I wanted to know was how I could stop the uproar within me as quickly as possible and get back to the fabulous living of my fairy-tale life.

The questions. All the questions …

The answers weren't simple. And they did not reveal themselves quickly.

---

The year in France was indeed an experiment. Life slowed down from the constant race and competition that it had been. I stopped working at the job I lived and breathed for nearly fifteen years (and other jobs before it). The kids began to gain their own independence in life and needed me less. We had moved far away from my parents, which freed me of some of their demands on my time and energy. My husband traveling for work internationally and both of us involved in interests of our own gave me time alone. I didn't have as much to juggle, manage, fix, take care of, and do. I suddenly had space and room to breathe. The distractions, which I had called "my life" for so long, started slowly to fall away, and what was left was just me. Me in this slower and beautiful place I loved. And without the roles I had played for other people, without who and what I was to everyone around me. I had no idea who was left. This new life in Paris, my new friends, my new interests, this city, and this newborn desire to do so much more than work and achieve—it all put me back in touch with a part of myself I once loved but no longer recognized. Who even was I?

Standing alone, by myself, in the middle of my life I, the warrior, trembled with terror. I felt lost, confused, and abandoned. I also noticed just how exhausted I was and had been for as long as I could remember. I did not understand it at the time, but the panic attack in St. Barths was my body breaking under the weight of it all, simply sending a clear signal that the way I was living was no longer sustainable and somehow not meant for me.

The crack in my outer shell—the "Marta" that I presented to the world and also truly believed I was—allowed for the old pain to start to surface. The belonging and love I started to feel in my community allowed for my body to finally feel safe enough for this process to begin. The way toward healing and freedom from my past was in those dark, painful, hidden truths that I had abandoned or simply wasn't willing to see because they hurt so much, in those early years of my life.

This was my invitation to the inner journey. Not exactly a gentle whisper. This was my soul knocking violently, after I had ignored her for too long, taking drastic measures. She stopped me dead in the tracks of my perfect Parisian life and brought me to my knees.

And there she asked me:

"Just what the fuck are you doing with your life?"

I was desperate to find out.

"There is more," she whispered. "Come and see …"

# The Inner Journey

# CHAPTER 9

# The Unraveling

When the panic attacks started in St. Barths and anxiety took me hostage in Paris, it was this whole story coming up to the surface. My painful past, the entirety of which I had hidden from everyone, started rising up from the abyss, where I had banned it to. I never talked about all of it. Not even my husband knew of the terror I lived with as a child. Not even I was fully aware of it: I had pushed it so far back into my subconscious that I forgot most of the details myself. The early memories I describe in this book only started coming back after months and years of therapy. They arrived like disjointed snapshots of scary experiences frozen in time—almost like old black and white pictures in a dusty photo album that hadn't been opened in a while. I repressed them all. What else could a little girl do with all that pain and fear?

I learned later that this is how the "trauma brain" works. As trauma victims, we "dissociate," leaving our bodies and living up in our heads, in our imagination, in order to ensure survival. The things we deal with are so painful that we cannot face or process them properly, and so we leave the present and disconnect from what's happening, from ourselves, from our bodies. It may look like we're there and we get quite good at performing tasks on autopilot, but later we don't remember much because we aren't really there. Realizing this a few years into my healing journey was both shocking and scary. How could I not remember? How could I not have more memories? I felt like I had lost that time somehow.

Later, I would see it as a gift that saved me. It prevented me from having to face something I wasn't capable of facing while so young. It was a beautiful way of protecting myself.

In place of memories, I painted a perfect picture of my childhood from stories my parents shared and the photos we kept from vacations and special occasions—the good times. I told people this version of the past because it was what I believed. How loving my extended family was and how much they meant to me and how I missed them and longed for my country, for home. I was open about how close I was to my parents and how we always leaned on each other in crisis. I spoke about the wonderful vacations, the silly times, the special celebrations, and our adventures together. Of course these were all true—they just weren't the whole story. I had erased the ugly parts of the picture because they were too painful: subconsciously blanking out certain things made it possible for me to cope. Immigrating made this easier to do, because it put a definite end to that "old" life. In order not to deal with the grief and loss of our departure, I banned all those experiences from conscious memory altogether. What I "chose" to keep intact (or rather what was subconsciously chosen for me) were the things I missed and wished for: a perfect view of a place called home, which never really existed. It set me up for longing for something I never really had, something ideal, also ensuring that I would never be able to attain it. I was forever longing and forever not home.

I also learned about something called CPTSD, complex post-traumatic stress disorder, and that it was something I carried. The complex part of the PTSD means that it happened repeatedly, over and over, so much so that it affected how my brain developed and how I perceived the outside world (as dangerous, in my case). I learned that the word "trauma" doesn't only refer to people who live through violent wars, horrific car accidents, or witness brutal murders. What I had experienced was trauma too: lack of safety, insufficient nurture, and feeling alone with it all (pretending to be brave on the outside when inside I was terrified) to the point of overwhelm. Trauma isn't only about what happens to you but what happens inside of you as a result of the events or environment you grow up in. Many experts now say that we are all traumatized in childhood to some degree. It's just a matter of where you fall on the scale and how much work is then needed to reconnect to yourself. The thing with trauma is that while you can repress the memories in order to forget the pain, the body keeps the score. These memories live in our cells, our tissues, our muscles ... Eventually, the body presents us with a bill. Time to settle up! This was what started happening in France with the panic attacks and paralyzing anxiety.

While I was very young, I embodied fear. It became a part of who I was and it lived in my nervous system, which is responsible for all our thoughts, actions, and bodily functions. Not only was the outside world a scary and dangerous place, as life taught me, inside of myself wasn't safe either. Fear was actually what was living me. It showed up as this energy running through me like an electrical current, this need to move and do, racing thoughts and constant worry, an inability to truly rest and be still. I became what's called "dysregulated" so early on in life that it was the only way I knew myself to be: overwhelmed, flooded, triggered, taken over by emotions and feelings I couldn't handle. So I avoided having to face any of those emotions or feelings, which meant that I had to constantly be on the run, physically and mentally. Slowing down in any form meant possibly facing something I didn't want to deal with. For most of us it's some form of pain from the past. Therefore, I lived in this fight-or-flight mode as my natural state, running on adrenaline, fueled by stress and chaos, constantly busy and multi-tasking brilliantly, always in a hurry to the next thing, my mind in overdrive, never ever sitting still. This way of being became my comfort zone not because it felt particularly good but because it was familiar. The brain will always steer us back to the familiar (even if it's toxic for our well-being) because the familiar doesn't signal danger—the brain recognizes it as something it already knows. It feels like home. It feels safe. All this served me well for years! I could manage a crisis like it was nobody's business at home and at work: always on, compartmentalizing, organizing, strategizing, executing all while keeping my feelings and emotions in check. It was almost like a soldier in a battle, not a woman living a life.

What I also learned as a kid was to constantly scan my environment for danger—part of the fight-or-flight way of living and another trauma response. I was always on guard while in the world. This is called "hypervigilance" and results in an oversensitivity to external stimuli like sudden noises and bright lights causing a jumpy overreaction driven by fear response. What I was also scanning was the body language and reactions of my loved ones at home. I wanted love, praise, and positive words, so I would mold myself into what they wanted of me and become it, which led to acceptance, compliments, and praise. It was a genius strategy of survival but it turned into years of people-pleasing and performing, not having any boundaries, self-abandonment, self-sabotage, and complete disconnection from who I was. Conditioned compliance comes at a high price: the loss of true self. I was only what others wanted or needed of me, and I only believed I was good at it if they received it well and told me so. This felt like love. It was unsafe to say "no," to speak up for myself, to express any form of differing opinion, or voice displeasure. I would do anything to avoid the discomfort I felt inside while finding myself in any form of a conflict, even a small and insignificant one, because for me conflict equaled abandonment. I couldn't cope with the tension I would experience inside of me, so I complied. And that felt "good."

The feelings of loneliness and abandonment were also a result of how I lived as a child. There was just so much danger outside and inside of me when I was so very little and nobody to help regulate or soothe me. This was, first, because I had no words to describe what I was experiencing while so young. I couldn't understand it myself, let alone share it with another. Second, my parents and other caretakers were all in their own state of survival. They too were experiencing trauma, danger, and fear—and trying to juggle it all—living life, raising kids, working jobs, standing up to the government, planning an escape from communism … It was a lot. There was no time for nurturing, for affection, for a tender holding that I so much needed. Besides, those were the days of "let the baby air out her lungs." No one was aware of the crucial skin-to-skin contact we now know helps babies regulate, soothe, and develop healthy attachment. So no adult had time or the capacity to be fully present, attuned, attentive, engaged, and connected to me. I always felt like a burden, like I wanted "too much" or needed something that I was not allowed to ask for, while there was just so much to do and everyone was so busy running around doing it. A deep longing ache developed within—to be seen, to be heard, to be validated. It made its home inside of me and ensured everywhere I went and everything I did would eventually end up making me feel abandoned and alone, because I carried it with me everywhere. I showed up expecting it and therefore unknowingly caused much of it myself.

By going all the way back into my childhood during and outside of therapy sessions, I examined what beliefs and agreements I was living under and who I thought myself to be. I asked where all of this came from—how much of it was my idea and how much of it was just passed down to me by others (to whom it was passed down by those who came before them and so on). I started to see how much of my present-day life was being driven by these old beliefs, that the world wasn't safe, that no one could be trusted, that I had to keep busy, that I had to be productive and work hard, that I needed to get everything done alone, that I had to be a certain way ... While all these served me well in the past and ensured my survival and success, I started to see that they simply stopped working. Rather than being helpful, they became a weight I carried.

Even though nobody was standing over me demanding that I comply, follow the rules, and "do it this way," it was all so ingrained in me that I held these expectations above my own head. My inner critic. My self-saboteur. My self-judgment. My own self-imposed cage. These old beliefs were now limiting me and preventing me from further growth. (We are not meant to stop evolving and maturing when we reach adulthood, by the way!) They were keeping me stuck in life, as I lived in survival mode and therefore continued living out of fear—either doing all I could to avoid it, fighting against it, or pretending it wasn't there: resisting, rebelling, or repressing it. Just like my parents. Just like their parents. Just like most people. With this understanding, I began to tell myself that I had already survived, that I was already safe. And at first it shocked me just how much nothing within me could or would believe it. So much evidence out in the world told me otherwise, so many bad things had happened!

But I learned that I had a choice in how to move forward. I could keep living while trying to avoid that old fear, or face everything that had happened and move on differently. I could continue to blame everyone and everything around me for what did or didn't happen. I could continue living constantly triggered by little things resulting in large overreactions and causing more suffering, not just for me but also to those around me. The alternative? I could decide to face my pain once and for all. Otherwise I would continue to pass it on. We either transform it or transmit it. I chose to stop the cycle—it would all end with me. I decided to spend time processing it all, accepting it, understanding it, letting myself feel the grief, the loss, the disappointment, the fear, the loneliness, the terror, and then take radical self-responsibility for who I would become after I let all that move through me. I realized just how much the past was holding me hostage. It was *who* I was. I was living my past story in the present moment unknowingly—constantly bringing it with me everywhere—which also ensured the future would continue along the very same path. The ending of the story was always the same (and predictable every single time): I will end up feeling abandoned and alone; no one can be trusted and the world isn't safe; bad things always happen; good things get taken away and I have to be the warrior to fight for survival; I have to always be brave.

All this started to sound familiar and I asked myself, *What if it is not actually true?* I didn't want my trauma to define me and who I was. I wanted freedom from it. I wanted it to become just a part of what happened to me, one small part of the whole big story. This was what took work. It was a complete change of my operating system, with very little guidance on how to do it at the time, just a deep knowing that something had to evolve, that something had come to an end, that something was in the process of dying. The repeated cycles of trauma (my own as well as generational) would end with me. I would do this not only for myself and my future but, most importantly, for my children, for their children …

What gave me huge hope was my self-education on trauma and the human brain development, mainly neuroplasticity, which says that no matter how your brain was wired as a child (your most important development actually happens before you're four as it helps to shape your view of the world and yourself in it), you can change it. You can actually rewire your brain and change the way you've been thinking and behaving. You can break the habit you call "being yourself." All of it is based on the past—your memories, thoughts, and experiences—leaving no space for anything new to ever take place. The past is constantly running our lives, and we don't even know it because 95 percent of the time we function on autopilot. We filter everything that happens with the lens of what's already happened to us, expecting to find evidence of what we already know (like that the world is a dangerous place and people can't be trusted so I have to be a brave warrior). The brain is always looking to make sense of our experience—and this makes sense! But it's the same loop over and over: the same unhealthy relationships, the same unsatisfying jobs, the same conflicts with our parents, the same issues in friendships, the same efforts to prove our worth, to prove we are loveable—always the same problems following us each time we move to a new city and promise that this time it will be different. It's always the same, in never-ending repetition.

Awareness is where the journey begins. I started to be curious about who I could become if I wasn't constantly living out of my past, my story, my habits, my patterns, the part of me that I thought was my personality. What if there were no limitations? What if there were no rules? What if I had a choice that came with complete freedom? What if I could break the cycles I was always finding myself in? Who would I be then?

My healing process started with facing the old fear, and it felt like anything but healing. Before I had any understanding of what was happening, I just felt afraid. Actually, I felt afraid of being afraid! It was such a strange thing because I had done so many brave and courageous things! I did not see myself as a person who was afraid. I had just moved to a foreign country, set up our kids in an international school, rented a new apartment in the middle of Paris, and gone through the process of selling our business, after over a decade of trailblazing and innovating in the online travel industry. A strong and fearless woman on a mission. I had accomplished so much in life and suddenly I found myself paralyzed by fear like a little kid afraid of a monster. It just made no sense! It wasn't until much later that I realized it was the old terror coming up to the surface. I wasn't afraid of anything in the present moment—this was the old fear being remembered. It had been stuck in my body and woven into the very fibers of my being, hidden within the depths of my soul, locked away in the dark corners of my heart, tucked in at my very core, and ignored for so long. Never to be opened. Never to be seen. Never to be revisited. *Silent. Forgotten. Fixed*, I thought.

This fear I believed I had banished forever when I was very young was asking to be seen, felt, held with compassion, understood and processed, in order to be integrated and then released. To make space for the new, I had to let go of the old. Not by repressing it but by feeling it all. The way toward freedom was right through the middle of that experience of pain and fear, but in order to be able to go there, I needed help. I needed guidance. Because once trauma is reactivated in your body, your logical brain simply goes offline. There is no telling yourself you're safe. There's no reasoning with yourself that all this is just silly, that you are not really in danger—it just *feels* like you are, because you're so hijacked by the old memories still very much alive in you that you cannot separate yourself from the experience of it. And the brain cannot distinguish the past from the present once the emotions start rushing through your body. Having such a flashback feels like being in the vortex of a hurricane of sensations, which is sometimes called flooding. The thirty-nine-year-old me experienced the fear of the six-year-old me in this way. I was absolutely unable to distinguish "then" from "now" and had no idea at the time of what was happening. My body was just signaling threat.

In Paris, I started seeing an American therapist who asked the right questions and let me cry in her office while she listened with compassion. It was very uncomfortable and I was so embarrassed to be such a hot mess and turn into a sobbing child right in front of her. I told her things I never shared with anyone and she understood me. She didn't tell me to be brave or to suck it up and power through it. She didn't remind me how lucky I was and to count my blessings. She didn't tell me of the many people who have it so much worse. She didn't correct me and say that my version of the story wasn't quite right, that I was not remembering it correctly. She didn't say that this was all for my good and what was best for me, that I would be able to see that later. She didn't recommend I try harder at being grateful by making lists of things I should be thankful for. She didn't judge me, yell at me, or tell me I was exaggerating or whining. She didn't say that God had a plan or that good would come of it. She just listened and heard me. I could see in her face that she felt the pain I was sharing with her. And seeing her hold my pain was like a magical potion for me. It was so loving that it moved me to tears. She truly saw me. Something inside of me opened up more. I think it was my heart, which had been so very broken for so very long and refused to trust anyone or let them get too close. I let myself be fully seen. It was possibly the riskiest move of my life. It was possibly what saved my life, or gave my life back to me.

It was my first time in therapy and my sessions began with a lot of tears. It was as if the floodgates suddenly opened and decades of sadness were running through me—it was physically and emotionally exhausting and required daily naps. I thought the crying would never end. Healing became my full-time job. I was unable to function otherwise. I didn't call it "healing" as there was nothing healing about it, or my expectations of what healing should feel like. Jim and I called it "mining" as it seemed each session I'd just go deeper and deeper into the past that I tried so hard to forget for so long. It was digging up old pain and sitting in it, completely counterintuitive. It really sucked. It hurt.

What we started working with first was breaking down the picture-perfect story I told myself about my childhood. My therapist could clearly see the hurt I was carrying and that something didn't exactly add up. We cannot heal what we cannot see, and she helped me to see that the way I grew up wasn't all that great. It actually wasn't even all that normal. Seeing my parents as real human beings with their own trauma, issues, and faults was very painful. It brought forward the grief of not getting what I needed as a child and many of our sessions were spent in role play, which I really hated. The grown-up me had to talk to the child me, and it made *all of me* extremely uncomfortable. It was what is called "inner child" work and also "reparenting," which helped me to get in touch with all that I was feeling as a child, as my little girl cried and cried for all the scary and terrifying experiences and the lonely times in Poland. The grown-up me would listen, comfort, love her, and then (and this was the most awkward part) tell her what she needed to hear (out loud!). I would switch chairs as I took on the role of each part of me—the child Marta and the grown-up Marta—and it felt super awkward and embarrassing. However, I was being the parent the little Marta needed in each of the instances of pain that I was starting to remember. It was brutal work. The old pain was so intense, some days I could barely breathe through my tears and didn't think I could make the hour-long journey home on the Parisian metro (often during rush hour and transferring at one of the largest train stations in the city). Fear made way for this sadness. Sadness made way for grief. Grief made way for anger. Anger stayed awhile and eventually made way for forgiveness. This part took the longest time—acceptance.

I studied breathwork after my therapist taught me a few breathing exercises, and I saw the difference it made in my body. It soothed and calmed me. I realized how much of the time I was holding my breath or sucking in my stomach, which created so much tension within my body. My muscles were always tight. My jaw was always clenched. My shoulders were constantly up around my ears. My posture was just a ball of stress and tightness. Breathwork taught me to open up and release some of this pent-up energy. This led me into an interest in yoga where I discovered how various emotions are stored in different parts of our bodies. I learned about human anatomy and how certain movement combined with breathing could not only regulate my nervous system but help release those stored emotions. And the best part was that you didn't always have to fully understand it all to release it—you could just breathe and cry and feel relief. I would find myself in hip-opening postures and simply sob. It felt so vulnerable but also fascinating that the body had this power and ability. I discovered that I had built up quite the armor, which I was carrying to cover up my pain and keep it all contained, and that it just became too heavy. While it kept me safe and protected, it also prevented me from receiving what I really wanted and needed, which was love. It kept the dark out, but it also prevented the light from getting in. It was time to work on taking my armor off and it felt terrifying. While what I wanted the most was to be seen, letting myself actually be seen was something I didn't know how to do. *Just be. Just breathe. You're not a human-*doing; *you're a human-*being. *Stop running. Just* stop. This was yet another foreign language I was learning. All of this was my yoga work along with learning that my body was a safe place for me to be, because once I slowed down and actually stopped, all I felt within me was being afraid. Feeling my fear was the scary part. This led to lots more crying—this time in yoga classes and workshops—but I continued on. Yoga brought me to trauma-informed or trauma-sensitive yoga, and I studied more deeply about the body "keeping the score" and how trauma affects us as children and adults. I got certified as a yoga teacher at the highest level as well as a trauma-sensitive yoga instructor, and this brought on a deeper understanding of my own pain and more memories started to surface. Nightmares came. Trouble sleeping. My panic attacks became worse. I started medication (an antidepressant) to help myself get up out of bed in the morning but I continued the work. It felt like things were getting worse rather than better and I wondered why I started digging into all this to begin with. I started trauma counseling. I studied and practiced meditation. I prayed and I continued crying. It did not feel "cleansing" or like a "releasing" most times. It just felt like pain, again and again and again. But I had no choice. There was no going back to "before" because it all stopped working, it all fell apart. I could not unsee what I had come to see and not "unlearn" what I had learned. I had to take small steps forward, as difficult as it was. I just placed one foot in front of the other. It felt gruesome and so slow. "Progress over perfection," I reminded myself.

Friends and counselors recommended books and I read everything. Books on the human brain and child development, how we attach to our primary caregivers (my mom and dad for me), and how it affects *all* of our relationships. Teachers and mentors and women with wise words showed up when I was ready and always said the things that pointed me forward—seeking more, searching and learning, thirsting for answers. I watched a video my husband showed me of Brené Brown talking about vulnerability. I had never heard that word before and learned all about shame and (un)belonging. It was so familiar but now I had words for the experience. I read everything Brené wrote and then more. The work of Richard Rohr, a Franciscan priest and spiritual teacher, introduced me to mysticism and the practice of contemplation. He completely changed my view of God and expanded my faith. I wanted a sacred encounter with The Divine of my own and I craved silence and solitude. In the moments when I experienced them—everything stood still. I read everything he published, and then I read some more. Spiritual journeys of others, psychology texts, self-healing books, prayer practices, meditative techniques, biographies of spiritual teachers of various religions and faiths, the Bible, writings of doctors, theologians, psychologists, scholars, yogis, priests, monks, philosophers and healers. This was where my "if they can do it, so can I" mentality was truly a blessing. I saw myself in many of these stories, which gave me hope and made me feel less crazy, less alone.

As if by divine timing (because I certainly believe it was!) right before my breakdown in St, Barths, Jim and I had signed up for a Bible study group in our new Parisian church. We volunteered to host it in our home over coffee and croissants every Friday, because that was back when I could still keep my shit together. I had never read the Bible from cover to cover nor been very involved in a church before. For me this was most importantly a promise of the presence of a family—the course lasted for over a year—and an opportunity to entertain guests and friends, which I always loved. Miraculously, our Parisian pied-à-terre filled with twelve people each week who were in constant prayer for me. While we stopped all our social engagements, parties, and dinners out, we kept our commitment to open our home to this group regardless of how I was feeling. Some days I couldn't make it downstairs from my bed but they still met in our space and filled it with love. Besides Sundays at church, this was the only time when we were around people during this season of our lives. Our apartment became a sacred space, a holy ground, and a container of love for me (and support for Jim) while I suffered through the worst of my crisis. These people taught me about community, connection, and love—not the kind that disciplines but the kind that offers grace. I learned that I could come broken—that *this* was the whole point actually—to come broken so that I could be loved and embraced for my messiness. Not some cleaned-up version of myself that I had been presenting to the world all this time. This changed my worldview completely. I felt relieved.

And so, of course. Of course this was when and where I broke open and unraveled. I finally started to feel safe. I started to feel seen and understood. I stopped pretending. I stopped saying "I'm *fine*. And how are *you*?" I came with my beautiful mess instead. I shared my broken heart. I spoke about my wounds. I no longer had to mold and shape myself into some acceptable way of being—it was okay to come just as I am—no mascara and puffy eyes from all the tears. There was suddenly permission to just be fully human. It was okay to come with my questions with my doubts, with my confusion, with my lostness. I could bring it all. For the first time in my life, I started to feel supported and not that I was the one supporting others. What really paved the way for the next phase of my healing were the women in my life. They held space for me, offered wisdom, provided encouragement, compassionately listened, tenderly cared for me, and prayed over me when no answers existed. They suffered along with me. They brought me flowers and took me for walks. They made me chicken noodle soup and wrote me love notes. They spoke truth in love. They called me out on my bullshit when I would try to armor up or mask up again. They pointed out when I'd call unacceptable things "normal." They got me out of my pajamas when I couldn't leave my bed and took me to coffee. I think I cried in every café in Paris that year. These women didn't run from my drama. For them, I wasn't too much. I wasn't a wreck to be avoided. I wasn't someone to be made fun of and gossiped about. I wasn't someone to medicate because I made them too uncomfortable. I wasn't taboo because perhaps I triggered their own fear and pain while I voiced mine. I was the brave one that spoke about the things most didn't dare to mention, but many of us questioned or experienced. The friendships I formed at that time were the deepest of my life. They were my lifeline.

It turns out that one of the biggest tools of healing trauma is community. Human beings are wired for connection. Love can do the impossible, after all, even heal childhood wounds. It was finally safe enough to go back. I was ready to see what had remained hidden for so long because I felt love, support, and safety all around me. Entering into this pain was my doorway in. It was the beginning of my transformation into something more than I had "been being" up until that point. It was the start of a journey to finding the real me underneath who I had become by conforming, surviving, and avoiding pain. Facing my childhood trauma and that old fear was just the first step. Once I learned to calm and soothe my body and my mind (with yoga, breathwork, and letting myself cry to my therapist and my friends), the panic attacks almost stopped. The fear was no longer leading my every moment by showing up and hijacking me from the present and flashing me back to the past. It still came and went but it was manageable and I wasn't so afraid of it anymore. I understood it. I had compassion for it, for myself. I still suffered from anxiety but it no longer paralyzed me. I continued leaning on others, reading everything, going to therapy, doing yoga, practicing meditation, and prayer. I surrendered into the loving care of my tribe and learned how to ask for help and accept it. Things stabilized and life seemed to continue its flow.

# CHAPTER 10

# Healing Trauma

ealing is like peeling an onion—it happens layer by layer and also comes with all the tears! A few years into my inner journey, just when I started to feel stable and steady, life brought us back to the United States. Having to leave behind my community in Paris, the home, and way of living which I loved, triggered another level of old pain. Even though I participated in choosing our relocation, fully agreed to it, and was excited about it, my immigration trauma was front and center when we arrived in Sarasota, Florida, in July of 2018. It was an invitation to go deeper. It was time to pull back another layer.

At first it blindsided me because I thought I was done. I thought I had arrived. I figured I was "healed." But then the pattern started to seem familiar: the cycle of deconstruction to reconstruction; disorientation to reorientation; breaking open to put the pieces together in a new way. A death leading to a rebirth, transformation. It was time to shatter another box I had been living inside of, which I outgrew, to let go of something old to make space for the new. Again. A lesson was here and, if I didn't run from it, also an opportunity to heal and expand some more. Understanding what was happening did not make it easier to deal with the same physical symptoms that paralyzed me in 2014. It was back to panic attacks and anti-anxiety medicine (after I had worked hard to wean off it and the antidepressant with the help of a psychiatrist in France). Somehow I knew this part of the journey I had to make alone:

some dark places one must visit herself. No girlfriends to hold my hand through it this time. No sacred friendships to sustain me and breathe life into me. I had this deep trust that I was taken out of my beloved community into isolation for a reason and that it would not be forever. As much as I had learned to lean on the support of others and ask for help, this time the invitation was to lean on and support myself, but in a new way, deep down on a soul level. While I found myself in Paris as a woman who is a part of a loving tribe, it was now time for me to find myself and who I was outside of the roles I played for others in my life. It was time for me to enter my own desert.

I found a local therapist and a yoga studio in Sarasota and began the process of talking about and moving through my immigration trauma. While I had somewhat made peace with and processed my upbringing and early years, it was the departure and running away from Poland, as well as the heartbreaking arrival in America that needed healing next. Both had a profound impact on who I was as an adult woman and how I moved about in the world, how I functioned, and who I became. It was time to answer the question I started hearing back in Paris but perhaps had needed a response upon becoming the "resident alien" in the USA at thirteen: Who was I? It was no coincidence that I was witnessing my son go through a similar process as he entered high school—also arriving from Europe into the American school system—his experience mirroring mine and triggering my own unresolved struggles and wounds.

I was a political refugee who fled my home country for safety as a teenager. Besides the danger and lack of safety that I embodied and had become aware of, this also meant I was homeless. The new life in my new homeland in America had some devastating beginnings. I wasn't welcomed. There wasn't freedom waiting for me as promised. I was uprooted and planted somewhere unfamiliar, a place that didn't want me filled with people who didn't like me. Because of this I felt that I never belonged; I was always the outsider, always the foreigner, always the stranger. I felt that the way I was wasn't acceptable or loveable, so I needed to fix myself in order to fit in. Marta needed a rebranding of sorts. I had to work harder than most at this self-improvement project because I came with a built-in deficit—I was worth less as an immigrant. I was the ugly duckling, the loser, the nerdy girl needing a massive makeover, and on top of all that I was a foreigner, which seemed to be a dirty word in the America I encountered. What people showed me by how they received and reacted to me at thirteen was evidence: I needed to become someone else. Marta wasn't enough. "I can do anything, become anything" was my motto. On the face of it, that shows self-confidence and optimism, but in fact it was my wounds and pain that drove me to succeed, the feeling of "not-enoughness" and worthlessness that fueled me to achieve. And it was here that I abandoned my true self for a persona I created and projected in order to fit in with the external world around me. I traded in my soul for the illusion of belonging. Which is why it became so exhausting and why everything eventually broke and fell apart. The pursuit of the American Dream came at the cost of losing myself in the process entirely—getting rid of my foreignness, erasing my roots, disconnecting from my essence and what made me uniquely me. This effort gave birth to my "hustle" or my "mask," my American me: the entrepreneur, the successful business woman, the strong leader. When that "me" had everything I ever wanted and expected the prize of praise, recognition, and a feeling of fulfillment, I got crash and burn instead.

I now know this happened because it was all unsustainable, a castle built on the sand of a false identity. The underlying goal of my pursuit of the American Dream was to make me feel like I was good enough. Nothing external can ever do that. There is absolutely nothing wrong with wanting more and pursuing success and all of your dreams and goals. However, if you think it will finally prove to everyone else (and to yourself) how amazing you are, you're in it for the wrong reasons. Like I was. I had been given signs that something was off all along, which I now call "the soul knocking," but I didn't listen. I just kept going, playing along, my eyes set on the prize—what the world defined as "having made it." My soul kept knocking louder and louder and I kept ignoring it, racing faster and doing more and doing it harder, until I was brought to my knees in St. Barths.

Oftentimes it takes a crisis in life in order for us to consider that perhaps there is more to life than how we have been living. For many of us, the soul has to take drastic measures to get our attention and finally stop us from rushing through life. This is especially often the case if we are successful, because our accomplishments and accolades give us the feedback that we are doing just great. And, by the outside world's standards, we are. But there is a whole other game at play in the meantime, which we cannot even see. When I started to really listen to the question, "Who are you?", really listen to what it was asking, I understood that deep down inside, I had no idea. I had lost myself entirely in all the "becoming." The burnout was an invitation to start looking at life from a different perspective and through a new lens.

This realization started my work of "individuation," which is separating yourself from your tribe and all the roles you play for others and truly connecting with your own identity, standing on your own two feet, and discovering a true sense of your cohesive self. It's taking away all the titles you identify yourself with and asking who you are at the core, then connecting to your values, beliefs, heart-felt desires and embodying them. This process normally happens in the teenage years but in my case, because this was when we immigrated, rather than going out in the world and exploring my identity, I clung tighter to my family because I had no safe base to move in or out from. The uprooting happened instead and so this important growth phase was stunted and I entangled and merged with my role within my family instead. It became who I was rather than discovering myself underneath.

I ventured into something called "shadow work" as part of my self-discovery. Shadow work is looking at the parts of yourself you find unacceptable or unattractive and bringing into the light the character traits that you like to hide from others (even from yourself) or the tendencies you have that you reject in yourself. If you aren't sure what those are, ask yourself what you dislike about the people who drive you crazy. You probably tell yourself you're nothing like them, and they annoy the hell out of you. Truth is, that trigger is asking you to see something in yourself. We are always mirrors to each other and the things that really get us worked up are trying to expose a truth we perhaps cannot yet see, one blind spot (we have many). Seeing your blind spots and developing a true self-awareness is brutal work. This is actually, and maybe for the first time, getting to know yourself—so that you can get to know your soul (who is the seat of who you truly are).

I added a life coach, spiritual director, and a somatic experiencing therapist to my support team and did a lot of journaling, regression (going into old memories), feeling old emotions in my body, and questioning the stories that came up in the process so that I could let it all go. (Was it really true, for example, that I was someone who didn't belong and didn't fit in? Was it true that the world is not a safe place and people cannot be trusted? Where have I seen evidence of the opposite?) It was disorienting at first because I was being asked to release everything I had learned about myself, life, and how the world functioned. But this was getting to the root of who I was (versus who I thought I was) and cleaning out the house to build a new foundation so that I could truly start over.

Because I didn't yet know who I was, I started with who I wasn't anymore. This led to saying "no" for the first time, being "unavailable" for certain things and to certain people, and setting boundaries. Boundary-setting sucks. Especially when you have never done it before. Lack of boundaries serves those around us really well—we always say yes and do what is asked of us! It usually comes from a good place—wanting to love the people in your life well—that was the case for me. But the one person we aren't loving when we have no boundaries is ourselves. When I started saying "no" or asking "why?" and losing the word "should," it really didn't go over well. I was told I was selfish, rude, inconsiderate, and bitchy. It also felt bad in my body. I was anxious about saying "no" and then I was anxious about the reaction to my "no." I had to deal with the guilt and shame that would come up after people did not respond well to my choices. I had to learn not to blame myself when this happened. It was a complete reprogramming of how I functioned and it was extremely uncomfortable (after all, I just wanted everyone to like me for all this time!).

Things between Jim and me got really tense, and I wasn't sure we were going to make it. I was suddenly changing the rules of the game on him, which led to his own lostness. He felt abandoned— his definition of how the world worked was partially based on me being a certain way and I was taking that away—but I wasn't willing to abandon myself anymore for the comfort of others. I also saw it as the most loving thing I could do for us as a couple, because if we were going to make it, this work was necessary. We needed to each heal individually before we could come together to cocreate something new and beautiful; something lasting and solid; a new kind of love based on freedom and not codependency. It was complicated, messy, and brought up a lot of old wounds and pain for us both. It felt like I was being unloving when I chose myself first. I felt selfish and self-absorbed. I didn't know how to do it gracefully. I made mistakes and screwed up often, I was learning.

My parents were also really confused by me stepping out of the old family dynamic and who they perceived me to be. I started voicing things I was unable to say in years, and it was clumsy and painful for us all. I felt so triggered by every conversation that I had to take almost two years of no contact in order to move through my process, not to become the little Marta in every encounter but find myself as the adult woman within our relationship. I couldn't find the words to tell them what was happening. I just needed space and time to be lost and drowning in it all before I could come back up to the surface.

It felt like I was fucking up and hurting people left and right. But I was determined to do things differently, and somewhere deep inside, I trusted that this would all work. Plus, there was simply no turning back. There was no going back to the old ways—they were what caused me to break in the first place. This was the transformation path I had read about so much, playing out in my very own life, just like the classic stories of the lives of mystics, seekers, and spiritual teachers. This was the only truth I hung on to: all this was somehow working out *for* me and not happening *to* me or *against* me. I had blind faith—because I needed to have something—I was letting go of everything else. It felt like falling into an abyss. But it was more than blind faith in reality. It was a "knowing" deep in my bones that this was my work to do.

I signed up for Intensive Trauma Therapy next and I flew out to Colorado, spending two weeks with a trained trauma therapist for up to five hours a day. I learned EFT (Emotional Freedom Technique, also known as tapping) and EMDR (Eye Movement Desensitization and Reprocessing), both intense techniques for healing PTSD. I spent a lot of time talking. This was the first time in my life I told my whole story, from beginning to end.

I will never forget the reaction of my counselor because he not only validated me but also gave me great relief. He said that after working with many clients for many years and hearing many stories, the thing he wanted me to hear was "Holy shit." He said it several times slowly just to make an impact, and it was at that moment I realized the full weight of what I had carried in my body. It was the kindest thing anyone ever said to me, and it wasn't even that nice. I cried for a very long time (most of our two weeks together) and just didn't see a possibility of the tears ever ending.

He used a word to describe my story and I still get chills when I hear it: "an orphan." Of course I had parents. Of course they loved me. Of course I had a family, even if distant and far away. But the foreignness and not-belonging that was so deeply rooted within me was contained in this one word along with my experience of the world. I understood that this was also ancestral. My father actually was an orphan, and some of the pain I was feeling was his. Perhaps even more was handed down to me further down our family lines, unintentionally. This is called generational trauma, which we all carry, whether or not we are aware of it. (At one time in history, Poland was completely wiped off the map for over a century. Talk about a lineage of homelessness and orphanhood! This story was in my cells too.)

My counselor and I looked at the coping skills and survival mechanisms I had developed, and I saw that some of them were amazing and helpful but some of them became unhealthy and limiting. We broke down everything I had put in place to survive. This was the most painful part. It felt like the person I had built up and become through all the energy and effort I put into keeping her alive was dying. I felt the grief. I felt my attachment to her— my personality—and the fear of what would happen if I let her go. Who would I be if I let her die? It was an intense process of life/death/rebirth, and I found myself in that space right after death but before rebirth. Like a caterpillar in a cocoon, liminal space of being held in the chrysalis. I hated the darkness, the stillness, and the waiting involved. A part of me didn't believe that I was held by anything. I didn't trust life completely, only sometimes, usually when things were going "well." The waiting to emerge transformed was agony and showed so clearly (yet again) just how hard it was for me to be still. My body couldn't handle it. The anxiety and panic attacks were so intense every time I tried to slow down. I didn't know how to sit with myself; how to just be inside my body, to just be. The storm raging inside of me was enormous. Again.

The cycle was familiar but I still kept losing myself in it. I couldn't see that it would pass like last time. I didn't believe it. I thought it would crush me. Some nights, I wondered if it would just be easier to die. I felt no separation between me—the one having the intense experience—and the experience itself. I still merged with my pain, my sadness, my fear. I became it. It colored everything all around me. I was suffering my way through it, still not knowing how to trust in that larger something orchestrating it all for me. I didn't yet know that I could be the one holding myself through it, while being held at the same time by something sacred and infinite.

What kept me going in those moments was love. It would somehow pop into my awareness and I'd think about my kids and how I would make it through all this for them. Because I wanted to see them grow and bloom. I wanted to break the cycles of trauma within our family and watch Mira and AJ be free of the pain and weight of it all. When you heal generational trauma, it is said you heal not just the generations forward, but also somehow, your lineage backward too. I would be the one. I was intentionally choosing this path, I reminded myself. I wasn't a victim of it. I was the brave, courageous warrior who would pave a new way forward for our lineage. I was a badass—the cycle breaker. It was a roller coaster of feeling like the most powerful human being on the planet and also the weak, helpless, small child waiting to be saved by someone outside of herself. The highs were high and the lows were low; swinging between the two—totally exhausting.

Before I returned home, I went to St. Barths for the third week of my therapy. I attended a yoga retreat where my job was to simply let everything I had learned in Colorado integrate. I didn't know what it meant, but my trauma therapist instructed me to stop reading, stop learning, stop ingesting new information, and just be present, let everything settle, and do things for the pure enjoyment of them. It was something I had forgotten in the midst of all my healing work.

I immersed myself in the beauty of the island and did yoga, breathwork, meditation, and journaling. I hiked. I swam. I ate gorgeous healthy food prepared by a plant-based chef. I went through the cycle of weeping and sleeping all over again, letting the pain move through me but this time feeling its exit, feeling the relief. The island held me with the beauty of its nature, healing waters of its ocean, and the magic of its sunshine.

I understood one day on a group hike the power of the story we tell ourselves about our experience. I was walking down a steep mountain and I was slow and tired. I felt clumsy and was questioning what I was even doing on this hike in such intense heat. The others were ahead of me and I started to feel that familiar shame of not being able to keep up, being left out, not belonging. Before my cycle of self-pity intensified, a new thought appeared out of the blue. *I'm not* by *myself. I'm* with *myself.* I paused, stopped walking, and smiled. Immediately I felt lighter on my feet and realized that I was choosing to keep myself company, to be present to and with myself versus keeping up with the others. I was choosing intentionally not to be with the group, and for me, it felt good to go slow that day, and this was okay. This was great, actually. What I was doing was honoring my needs in that moment, rather than getting in line with everyone else's pace. This was huge—realizing how I had done this often in life. The simple phrase "I am *with* myself" brought me deep joy. It was almost like a part of me was so happy and thankful that she was no longer abandoned. *Wow*, I thought. *How long have I been the one abandoning myself?*

I replaced "I am by myself" and the negative feelings it stirred up with this new statement. It became a new belief, which then became my truth. And then I wondered where else I could apply the same technique I had just stumbled onto. What else was just a story I was telling myself where I simply needed to change and update the context? What other lies was I subconsciously believing and clinging to for dear life?

Back home, I woke up one day and stopped looking for the tension, headaches, ringing in my ears, fogginess in my brain, muscle tightness, pain in my chest, and shallow breathing. I stopped anticipating just how badly I would feel upon waking. I decided this also wasn't working for me anymore. It was as simple as that. A choice. I somehow became aware of the victim cycle I was sometimes stuck in. It was just an awareness and then a decision to do something differently. While it is amazing and courageous to go to the depths of one's wounds and befriend them, we are not meant to hang out down there forever. It was time for me to climb out from the darkness and heaviness into some much-needed light and lightness; the retreat in St. Barths gave me a glimpse and a taste of this.

So I began each morning by intentionally spending a few minutes being thankful for another day, my warm bed and comfortable house, my family, my dog, my body and my breath, my heart. which had loved so much and also held so much pain. I just gave thanks. It felt forced at first, but each morning I would again begin this practice I had committed to. Be mindful. Be aware. Wake up and don't pick up the iPhone right away. Open my eyes. Be here.

Slow down. Take a few breaths. Pause for a few minutes. Pet Daisy (it releases the feel-good hormones serotonin and oxytocin, I read, and I was all about that!) and only then get out of bed. I started to see how much of my life was spent hurrying up so I could do the next thing. Brush my teeth so I could shower. Shower so I could get dressed. Get dressed so I could have my coffee … Like life was just checking boxes on a "to do" list while always in a hurry, and always running out of time.

I understood that if this continued, I would never really be fully present anywhere because I would always be thinking about what's next, what needs to get done. And so I slowed down and started paying attention to the things I was doing routinely and habitually—just by bringing myself to each moment I was in— when I could remember to do it. It wasn't all the time, it wasn't even most of the time, it was just sometimes, and that was okay. I kept practicing the skill of staying in the present moment and connected to my body in my daily tasks so that when there were triggers, I would know what to do: not get swept up in them but stay present and grounded instead and witness them. When I caught myself "being up in my head" and distracted—by thoughts, worries about the future, or reliving something I had done the day before that I didn't like—I would pause and come back to what I was doing that very second. Steaming the milk for my latte. Blow drying my hair. Washing the dishes. Walking the dog. Constantly shifting my attention where I wanted it to go, not letting it go where the mind wanders off to when left unattended. I kept coming back not just to the task at hand but also fully taking up space in my body. Feeling my feet on the ground when I was standing, my back on the chair when I was sitting, walking with intention when I was moving, mindful of every step. I became what I was doing.

*The answers are all within*, I heard while meditating one day. It wasn't a loud voice speaking from the sky or a soft tender whisper inside, like in the movies. It was inaudible. The sentence popped into my head out of nowhere, and I just knew it was true. This led me to go even more deeply into reconnecting with my body. I didn't know what "within" meant just yet but I knew I was heading there next.

We live so much by the intelligence of the brain. Everything is calculated and determined by thinking, deciding, analyzing, and spending lots of time in our heads: logic. It is praised, rewarded, and celebrated. We barely come up for air! If we happen to get tired of thinking in our brains, we look to our devices to figure things out: the "smart" phones. We ask Google and Siri. But what about the intelligence of our bodies? I wanted to stop overthinking, understanding, and processing everything and to get in touch with my intuition, my gut feeling. Furthermore, I wanted not just to feel safe in my body but connected and aligned with my feminine nature. I wanted to live out of the embodiment of a calm and peaceful energy I started to encounter inside myself during my meditation practice rather than reasoning/thinking/rationalizing. I wanted a softness, a flowing, a tenderness to my life, almost like a graceful dance. Not rigidity and rules, schedules and to do lists. The planner and organizer suddenly got sick of her agenda and lists. I wanted to throw my calendar out the window, and so I did. It felt fucking great, like I was unchaining myself.

I started experimenting with somatic therapy, which taught me how to be with what's moving through the body without freaking out or making it mean anything or needing to control it or get rid of it. I was learning safety in my own body and it was hard work for me—sitting with the discomfort while being aware of it and present to it. I always wanted to escape it, to run away from any pain or difficult emotion, to numb it immediately. My idea of allowing it was suffering through it with clenched fists and eyes shut waiting for it to pass. But I was being asked to be with what was happening in my body without getting lost in it, judging it, or telling myself a story about it. *This is bad. This is probably a heart attack. I don't like this. I feel like shit. I am really struggling. This will probably be the thing that kills me.* These were all my favorite stories to make up about a simple pain or tingle in my body if it stayed longer than I decided was acceptable. I had no capacity to sit with my emotions, to actually *feel* them when they showed up as physical sensations in my body. Little by little, I learned it is simply energy in motion and if we can just observe it move, eventually it passes. You cannot think your way into healing; you have to feel your way in. But we are trained to run away from discomfort, to numb it, to escape it, to medicate it. I never ever wanted to sit with any of it and actually ask it if it had something to show me. Could my pain also be my teacher? It sounded ridiculous but I started looking at things this way—symbolically, mystically, with a much wider lens. I welcomed the mystery of life and suddenly started to see just how little I knew or understood about how to be a human. Nobody taught me how to be in my body, to connect to my heart, to experience feelings in a safe way. It was so brand new and fascinating.

I journaled regularly and gained self-awareness of my own patterns of behavior and tendencies. The goal was to get to a space of not reacting to pain and triggers but finding a sacred pause then breathing into it in order to take action from a grounded and aligned place. The ability to sit with tension or discomfort in the body allowed for that energy to shift and move, after fully experiencing it being present, and then I was able to respond to a situation with full awareness of my actions and words. This was very different from feeling swept up in the drama of what was happening and out of control (the past taking over the present or the mind running with a story of what it all meant). There were moments when I found this impossible to do (like most of the time, at first!).

But I stumbled into something I coined "radical responsibility," and when those moments came and I did act out of an activated wound and snapped at someone because I was flooded with feelings I could not tolerate, I came back and apologized. I learned not to blame everyone else around me or to wish them to be different or change. I came to understand that my job in life is to be fully responsible for how I show up and who I am. This is my work but also my power. And this was also my path to freedom. Having a choice in every situation and knowing that this was true. I stopped giving my power away to everyone I was in relationship with—my husband, my kids, my friends, my clients, my parents, my business partners, the checkout guy at Whole Foods. The only validation I needed was internal. The only approval I was seeking was mine. Other people still mattered but I stopped being dependent on being needed, praised, complemented, recognized, rewarded, or looked up to. Their reaction to me did not determine my value. I was learning to know my own worth. I was learning to own myself. This felt extremely powerful in my body. I felt the strength of my back at the same time as the softness of my heart. I embodied both: fierce power and tender love.

And with that, I stopped looking for answers outside myself. A few church sermons about self-sacrifice for the sake of love, recommending I quietly submit and serve others more, brought up so much anger. What a disempowering and retraumatizing message for trauma survivors! On top of that, I felt the message was directed at women and wondered why men weren't given the same directives. And what about loving ourselves and not just our neighbors? As women we constantly live other-focused and pour out from an already empty cup. Why are we so judged and defined by our actions—what we *do*—and not just who we are. Does that mean if we don't do anything for anyone, we are worthless? Why are all my girlfriends also exhausted and resentful? My eyes were suddenly opened to how much we are oppressed by what we are told to do, how we are told to be. How men are told to be and what to do as well—the toxic overpowering masculine and the victim disempowered feminine story fed to us all by society. I couldn't unsee it. I got so sick of trying to live up to expectations. I found myself angry with everyone. Angry with my parents for training me how to be a "good girl" and setting up all the rules so early on in my life. Angry with my teachers disciplining me into being a "good student." Angry with the books I read and TV shows I watched as a little girl that taught me fairy-tale stories about romance, what love was, and how to be a "good woman" and a "good wife." I was pissed at the culture that wanted me to stay forever young, sexy but not too slutty, intelligent but not a know-it-all, assertive but not bitchy, successful but not too greedy, leading but not too bossy. I resented all of it—and how acceptable it was to strive for these impossible and unattainable goals. I was angry with the women who continued playing along and competing against each other in this fucked-up game. I was frustrated that they couldn't see the setup—pitting us all against each other. How disempowering! Divide and conquer. Because if we came together instead and stood shoulder to shoulder as sisters, what a powerful fucking force we would become in the world! I was most of all angry and disappointed with myself that I bought into all of this shit and spent so much of my life comparing, competing, and becoming all the things. I desperately wanted to *un*-become. But I didn't want to implode or explode on those I loved the most. I didn't want to blow up my whole family in the process. I didn't want to lose them. I might have been questioning everything else, but the one thing I knew for sure was that I loved them dearly.

I read a lot of spiritual texts and ventured into the landscape of soul and energy work next. I learned about the soul as a castle and how to intentionally enter that sacred space within and connect with my own heart: my inner temple, my sanctuary. I found profound peace each time I tried this and gentle tears would flow down my cheeks. This time when I got curious about the crying, I found that the tears weren't of sadness or pain. They were calm and beautiful tears of feeling the presence of love: I was moved by experiencing love within me. I studied the false self, the real self, the ego, the splitting off from our souls, and how we often abandon our true nature for the culturally acceptable versions of ourselves. This is why so many of us feel lots or disconnected and end up in jobs we hate, or relationships that aren't the best, or living in cities we don't enjoy. We do the thing that makes sense on the outside. We take the logical steps that come from the brain and thinking. We do not do the thing that brings us joy or lights us up inside, which is driven by our hearts and deepest desires. In those moments, and in moments of trauma, we split off from our true selves. We walk around in pieces, disowning and abandoning parts of ourselves. And so I played around with an idea of reclaiming my lost selves and calling them back in order to fully integrate them into wholeness. I understood just how fragmented I was living, dividing my life into sections and compartmentalizing the person I would become in each chapter. They were all so separate ... not one Marta fully merged and wholly herself. I wanted wholeness. Wholeness and acceptance—self-acceptance. Maybe even self-love. Maybe the gentle tears were the first experiences of softly beginning to love myself. I welcomed them.

A certain image kept coming back to me during this time, which I began calling "soul retrieval." I was driving a white school bus—my present-day self. I know it sounds strange, but stay with me. As I drove this bus, I picked up passengers along the way—all the old versions of myself that I had abandoned—from the crying infant, to the clingy three-year-old, the afraid six-year-old, the scared twelve-year-old running away, the thirteen-year-old who arrived and was bullied and crushed, the lonely teenager trying to survive, and the young woman finding her way in college and her early twenties. As I wrote each part of my story for this book, I welcomed that younger part of myself onto the bus, introducing her to the others, making her feel wanted, loved, and safe. They were all invited. They were all seen. They were all wanted. They were all safe and secure. There was no need to be angry, ashamed, guilty, embarrassed at any of the versions of myself. I was proud of them for how well they survived and how far they had each come. I thanked them. I no longer needed to hide them away. This was the first time that all fragments of me were welcomed all together, and I was teaching them belonging. I wanted to hear their stories, hold space for their pain, comfort their fears and worries so we could all come together into what I was hoping was wholeness, integration, my true self, the very essence of who I was created to be—not hiding or repressing anything. As I wrote about each part of myself, I let myself go back in time, imagine the place where I had been living at the time, and remember what I looked like back then from old photos. I fully brought myself back there as much as I could. What was I thinking, feeling, wearing, watching, eating, and experiencing back then? I would go to bed at night asking, *What else would you like to share? What else do you have to say? What else needs acknowledgment?* and I would wake up remembering more stories and jot them down in the notepad I kept at the side of my bed. I would play the music I listened to in those times of my life and write some more—write and cry and feel the pain of the life I was describing, feel the loneliness, confusion, sadness, grief, shame, and constant separation from others. I would let it all come over me and tears would flow, and I would hold it gently and kindly as my body felt what the younger me had no capacity to experience. I would breathe into this space I was creating for myself and sit with the old feelings I had been running from for so long. And as I watched them come and flow through me, I would also eventually watch them go. Then exhaustion and release would hit and often I would have to stop writing and rest, sometimes for days at a time. Sometimes weeks. This was my healing. I had finally slowed down long enough and gone inward deep enough for all this to unfold before me. I had developed the capacity to sit with the feelings that once traumatized me. It felt like purging or purification of some kind—letting the old things go—old stories, old versions of myself, old fears, old habits, old wounds, old feelings that still held me hostage. Intuitively, I completely trusted the process and as I soothed, comforted, and healed the younger parts of myself. I also called forth the new woman in me to emerge—a pleading, an invitation, a summons—to the woman I was meant to be but whom I had lost along the way when I started pleasing others and meeting expectations. I asked for my soul to be freed. I poured my heart out on paper, typed the words on a keyboard, spoke the most vulnerable things I could find in the depths of me, and I let myself be led to the next thing. Eventually I figured out where the white school bus was heading. It was taking me —all of me—home. Home to myself. I was on a journey of homecoming.

*What if home and belonging had nothing to do with where I was located physically, where I lived and who I hung out with?* I wondered. *What if home and belonging were also an inside-out job?*

The moment I asked this, I knew it was true.

All this work was really tiring so besides a lot of naps, I really started to need massive self-care. I came from the old-school way of thinking that self-care was a luxury and a waste of time—neither of which I was interested in because I deemed them unproductive. But the release I felt in my muscles from a simple massage was noticeable even on my face. When I left acupuncture and felt like the weight of the world wasn't on my shoulders anymore, I saw significant changes in how I was able to interact with others. When reflexology gave me the ability to breathe deeper and feel more rooted and balanced, I started going regularly. Bodywork became a huge tool in healing all the stress and trauma I carried. It allowed me to soften and melt the tension I carried within my muscles, fascia, tissues, organs, and cells—it was everywhere! So, I saw osteopaths, sound healers, physical therapists, energy workers, shamans, you name it. I left no stone unturned. I was all in.

They were not all wonderful experiences and this was definitely an experiment, but I was willing to try anything once. Healing is an extremely personal journey, and this taught me how to listen to my body and to trust myself even more. Excellent (but not trauma-informed) psychotherapists would retraumatize me by trying to go back to memories that were too overwhelming, wanting to keep talking and talking about the pain. Unqualified life coaches would go too fast or too rough into certain spaces, and I would recoil and feel triggered and betrayed. Self-proclaimed expert meditation teachers tried to make me sit still and quiet in lotus pose when I really needed time to move first, to get used to the space of stillness and silence. I needed to downshift my gears before I could ease into meditation and not be anxious. Inexperienced breathwork facilitators would walk me through practices that brought on panic attacks rather than soothing my nervous system.

Healing trauma is very much about establishing safety first, and then moving in and out of the overwhelming experience. Toggling between the safe space and the trauma. Gentleness and a kind holding are required. Tenderness and compassion are key. So many people try hard but yet don't understand this: with trauma, it's not try *harder*, it's try *softer*. Sadly, several acupuncturists and masseuses didn't feel safe to me, because of how they approached my body. Certain yoga teachers continued to come up from behind me or stand over me to give adjustments, which only triggered me. Each time I was like a little kid running back to the corner of her dark room alone to cry with the old fear that would crop up yelling, *How could you?! I trusted you!* It was really painful.

But then I became my own protector. I would speak up in those cases and walk away from what didn't feel good or stop attending group yoga classes. It really taught me to stand up for myself, to say "no" more often, and to choose what worked for me and what didn't. This was also a lesson in gaining my power back yet again. In those experiences I stepped out of the victim role I played: being the one who felt she entrusted herself to the supposedly capable hands of experts, who only damaged her further. These well-meaning people never asked to have that kind of power over me. It was not their job to rescue or save me. What sometimes felt like taking five steps backward to take one step forward taught me to give this kind of power to myself only. Only I could save and rescue myself in a way that led to true, lasting freedom. This was the ultimate cure for a trauma victim: having a choice, having a voice, and having access to the power to facilitate my own healing. In all these ways, I was constantly coming back and checking in with my soul about what was the right decision for me and what felt good in my body. This was how I started to connect to my true self. This was how I first started to meet her.

# CHAPTER 11

## Finding Freedom

The more I peeled back the layers of the onion and continued my healing, the more that visual started to morph into another. The initial layers, the outer shell of me, was the pain, the old trauma: my hard edges of self-protection, coping mechanisms, and survival. Once I got through those veils, it was like pulling back one curtain after another to see more, to actually get to know myself versus who I had become by following rules, accepting my conditioning, and living old patterns and trauma responses that kept me stuck in a loop. Since I learned that the persona I had developed and projected wasn't really the true *me*, the peeling of the layers changed in nature. It no longer was a desperate effort to fix and change myself into some healthy, cured, perfected, good-enough version. It was as if the onion had suddenly become a rose, and rather than peeling off the layers, I was simply opening up its petals to see what was hidden deep inside—or maybe who was hidden there … I was mining for diamonds, knowing that at the center of the rose, I would find one that shone brightly, just waiting to be discovered, ready to emanate her unique light. It was my true self, my essence, my heart. Hidden under the ugly, stinky onion was a beautiful, fragrant flower that contained the treasure of my own soul. And suddenly the healing became a bigger and deeper journey of self-discovery, self-love, and self-revealing.

Starting to discover (or maybe uncover) myself and listening to my own body led to completely changing my diet: eating intuitively, taking supplements and herbs, and intermittent fasting and even getting certified as an integrative nutrition and holistic health coach. I started to see just how much my food choices were also a way to numb what I didn't want to face and how little I understood about what I ate: how it was made and where it came from and how it affected my body, my brain, my mood, my overall well-being. As I began to feel and release the pain I was running from all this time, weight started to come off my body. "Eating my feelings" was a funny phrase I had used for years along with "drowning my sorrows" when I'd crave carbs and give into several slices of pizza or drink an extra glass of wine when stressed. Processing and working through my trauma resulted in releasing so much of what I had been carrying. Emotional pain, stuck energy, old ways of functioning, loops and patterns ... became the heavy armor I carried. For me, this release was also physical and resulted in my body completely changing shape, physically shedding the false layers of protection it had built up to keep me safe. These extra pounds were also a way of hiding the diamond inside, of obstructing the light within from shining out. I was afraid to take up too much space, to attract too much attention. I was afraid to fully put myself out there. So I hid inside. I gave thanks for this safety and committed to fueling my body with healthy food to allow my flower within to bloom and eventually to fully open. I made conscious, educated, and intentional choices about what I was consuming to nourish myself, knowing that it can either work for me or against me. I understood that my body is a sacred vessel and saw just how poorly I had been caring for it for so long. I took it for granted and was always criticizing, shaming, pushing, and abusing it. I started to be thankful for the miracle that my body actually was, and paying attention to how I thought and spoke about it. I wanted to change how I saw myself in the mirror: I wanted to see only love and to feel only love for my reflection.

I wasn't there yet but I became aware of not just the type of food I was consuming but also the environment around me. Integrity — the way I was being in all areas of my life—became very important. Everything was intentional and something I was choosing for myself out of love and the honoring of my sacred life. I wanted to surround and fill myself with love only.

"You can't be just a little bit in alignment," a mentor said to me. "You are either aligned with who you are or not."

This felt like truth and I wanted to fully align with love. So I took inventory of how I spent my time, where I directed my attention, whom I met with, the places I went, what I watched on TV, and what I consumed on social media and read online. I decided to only allow good things in and around me, knowing that in order for the rose to blossom and open, she not only needed to be watered well and planted in nourishing soil, she also needed an environment around her that allowed her to flourish. It was all important. Unknowingly, I was starting to learn how to care for my own field of energy. A lot of my journey looked this way—I would start doing something intuitively because it felt good and right, not understanding what it was or why I needed it. I trusted those nudges, later reading somewhere that what I had stumbled into was a healing or spiritual practice. I let my body and my heart lead the way.

I started to stick closely to a morning practice that made me feel good to start each day —tuning in and getting in touch with my heart first thing. It made me feel slower inside and more confident of my connection to that sacred something within me, my own heart. This led to deeper trust and a more balanced and harmonized way of being and living. It was like something inside of me downshifted and slowed down drastically, no matter what was happening on the outside. I found that I could even be in a hurry externally while being slow and intentional inside. This morning routine became my ritual and a nonnegotiable, which helped me get into a sacred rhythm of my life and its seasons. (Just like nature has spring, summer, fall, and winter, so do we!) It made me feel at ease with the ups and downs of life as they happened around me. I was learning to ride the waves of the ocean called life. The idea wasn't for the waves to stop, but to gracefully live through both the calm waters and the stormy seas. I lit candles and incense, read spiritual texts, journaled about what came up, meditated, and listened to chanting.

By the time Covid hit, two years after arriving in Florida, Jim and I called ourselves "everyday monks" and were already living in self-imposed isolation. He was in his third year of sobriety after rehab and taking classes in an online seminary school. My husband was pursuing his path of a spiritual director for Caron, the facility where he got sober. I was on a spiritual journey of my own trying to pull back the layers/petals and find my own center, to unveil the diamond of my soul and stay connected to my heart. Our morning coffee conversations were always about spirituality and usually about mysticism—the personal experience of God / the Sacred / the Divine—and what we were both learning about it. We didn't have much of a social life in Sarasota so distancing from others wasn't hard once it became required. But the inability to travel made me have to sit even more still—*slow down* even more. I had grown used to traveling back to Paris to recharge my social battery and reconnect with my soul sisters. I still missed my friends and community there. During the pandemic's stay-at-home orders, I started traveling to new and exciting places inward, within me. It sounds crazy, but the journey can be quite adventurous if you are willing to leave the comfort zone of where, how, and who you currently are. I saw it as another sacred pause, time for reassessment and a shift in my life, like the initial panic attack in St. Barths, the breakdown in Paris, and the move to Sarasota. Each of those times allowed for an unmasking, a layer of healing, a deeper self-awareness and self-discovery. This time, the forced interruption in how I functioned, the fear and trauma it caused and triggered, were on a global scale: it affected everyone, not just me. I felt it deeply and heavily. I ventured deeper into my soul, exploring the space of the divine feminine, the desert mothers and fathers, the wisdom of the ancient cultures and Indigenous people, writings of Buddhist nuns and Christian monks. I shared it all with my husband, which led to really intimate and spiritual conversations between us. We were getting to know each other all over again, maybe for the first time. I worked with a private meditation teacher, one-to-one energy and vibrational healer, a shaman and body worker, and continued journaling and writing. I let my soul take the lead and got in touch with a different side to God than what I was taught, a God who poured herself right into me and told me that I was sacred and whole. That we all are sacred and whole. That we just forgot this truth and wander around searching for something "out there" to make things right when the treasure is, and always has been, the last place we'd look: inside ourselves. We are sacred at our core, not broken, and the journey of the soul is simply to remember this.

My idea of God / Divine / Beloved / Universe / Source (fill in your own term) grew bigger, beyond all human reasoning and understanding, filled with mystery, wonder, and awe. My faith deepened. My view of the world expanded. I was suddenly comfortable with just how much I didn't know about any of it. And that felt right. Life was a beautiful mystery, and I was enchanted with it all. I wanted to be able to watch it magically unfold in front of me without controlling it, fearing it, or attaching to the outcomes. I encountered a sacred text called *The Cloud of Unknowing* and everything became symbolic, mystical, mythical, and sacred. My heart was suddenly excited and curious about life. It was love that facilitated this shift. It is always love that motivates the soul to grow and evolve, like a magnet pulling it to its source. The sacred potion in my transformation was the beginning of feeling loved, deeply at my core. I started to truly open my heart and let myself feel it. It moved me to tears. I became aware of the beauty all around me and it moved me to tears too—colorful flowers, birds singing, butterflies, the way trees would swing in the wind, old people holding hands and babies running to their mamas—it all touched something so deep inside of me, awakening something within. It showed up as soft, gentle tears, which I welcomed.

I held online breathwork and meditation classes for friends in Paris stuck in small apartments during lockdown. There was so much anxiety and panic in the air, and I had found tools that helped me and wanted to share them with loved ones. I started teaching the slowing down, tuning in, and connection to one's heart, which I myself had discovered. It made me feel safe, quiet, and at peace, and it filled me with love, the kind of love that emanated from my own soul and was divine in nature. The kind of love I could access anytime if I just chose to slow down and turn inward, regardless of my external circumstances. It seemed like the perfect time because of the crisis we were all suddenly facing together. "Be still and know," I told my students and friends. "Be still … How can we ever expect to hear what God is trying to say when we don't get quiet enough?" I asked them. "How can we ever hear anything when so much of our prayers are spent asking and talking? Be still …" I reminded them, "You are safe. You are seen. You are loved. Be still and take a moment to simply receive this truth and feel it in your body. Be still …" I retreated from the world even more to slow down yet again and listen to the whispers and callings of my soul. The stillness and silence I had been encountering suddenly became pregnant and rich with messages and lessons. I started saying yes to those internal invitations (like starting the meditation sessions online when I felt completely unprepared and unequipped) because I trusted them.

The more I did, the more I heard them and the louder the voice became. I was developing self-trust and finally, at last, finding my true self: my identity, my essence, the truth of who I was. She was leading me. My intuition and inner knowing strengthened. I remembered my "I can be anything; I can be anyone" motto and wondered why it took me so long to simply be myself. But it was because I didn't know that who I was being wasn't actually me. I didn't even understand that sentence. I thought all of my actions, behaviors, jobs, roles, titles, thoughts, and feelings added up to this one big thing called *me*. I was so attached to all those externals because they became my identity. Here is the key idea that blew my mind. All those things were actually covering up the real *me*. I couldn't find her under all the distractions and noise of who I had worked so hard to become and who I thought myself to be. All my masks. Starting a relationship with my soul simply by connecting to it regularly was where I found myself—my true essence, the *me*—under all the stuff. This became not just a spiritual practice but also my life's purpose—to live connected and soul-led—as the pandemic swept across the globe.

---

"Let go," I started hearing. "Surrender and let go. Trust in the unknown."

I heard it everywhere. I saw it in huge signs, heard it in songs, and read it in every book I was plowing through. I hated those words. They signified weakness, helplessness, and choicelessness, which to me was how I experienced my early-life trauma. They meant disempowerment. And while the mind was busy trying to resist the idea, the body knew and the Universe would not rest until I learned this lesson: "Let go."

Jim, AJ, and I were lucky enough to get on the island of St. Barths for a few weeks during the lockdown while the island was open for a short period of time. The house we rented had a gigantic sign on the living room wall. "THE UNKNOWN" it read. I chuckled when I saw it.

"Okay, okay, I get it." But I did not. Not yet.

A week into our stay we learned that Mira, who was studying (and in lockdown) at Indiana University, had Covid. It was the early stages and the first wave of the virus when people were still dying from it in frightening numbers. I was petrified. Mira suffers from asthma so she was considered very high risk.

I heard, "Let go. Let go. Trust," again and again and again. I couldn't do anything to fix this. I couldn't do anything to help her. It was as if I was watching myself wanting to freak out but something was pulling me away from the chaos trying to sweep me along with it. Something kept me back and firmly grounded instead. I prayed. I meditated and visualized her body healing. I sent her vitamins and supplements and I texted her too often asking how she was feeling. I swam, moving my body through the water while worst-case scenarios moved through my brain. I tried to release them with each stroke and exhale. I let the sun comfort me and soothe me, cried on Jim's shoulder, and just put one foot in front of the other while she was sick and so far away. I worried. A lot. I felt helpless and scared, but I didn't kick into my normal overfunction mode to fix and control the situation. This created immense discomfort and anxiety within me. The magnetic pull of the chaos was intense but I was simply feeling it in my body (along with all my fear) and not reacting. This was surrender, a true test of it. Surrendering to the fact that this unpleasant thing was here and it didn't feel good at all. Surrendering to the circumstances that life was presenting without trying to manipulate them. Day by day and very slowly, Mira got well. Day by day I started letting her go and trusting that she could handle this herself, and that allowing her space to do so was actually loving her well. It was trusting in her and her own abilities to get through a challenging situation. It was the most empowering thing I could offer my daughter. Not to project my fears and discomfort onto her, but to support and love her as she found her way through her own crisis. I started accepting that all of it was completely out of my hands and my control. I was feeling the unknown. It was like stumbling in a dark long tunnel with no ability to see the exit or the next step in front of me. My only job was managing my own walk on this path, not controlling Mira's. My task was dealing with the fear that was triggered within me without projecting it onto her in frantic attempts to fix and manage. Letting go of her kids is a mother's hardest work. It is the hardest part of loving them well. But it is essential if they are to learn to stand on their own two feet, know who they are, and have complete trust in themselves. Releasing them to fly and soar on their own was the most challenging because I clung to them the tightest—I loved them so much. I had planted the seeds while raising them, now it was time to sit back and watch them bloom in their own time and in their own way. Giving them space and freedom while holding them in a field of love and being "home" to them, a safe base to move in and out of the world from.

During the second week on the island, I went for a hike with AJ, excited to show him some natural pools I recently discovered. We reached the beautiful spot, and the two of us jumped in. The previous time I'd visited them they were like a lake, completely still and calm. This time, however, a wave came and pulled me under with strength I had not experienced before in the ocean. I came up for air only to swallow tons of water. I could feel AJ struggling to reach the surface next to me, his hand brushing against my body as he pushed the water away. The terror of losing him shot through me like an electric current.

*What the fuck was I thinking?! I caused this. I brought him here. So fucking irresponsible!*

I fought the current and the "washing machine" effect it created, struggling against the power of the water until I had nothing left in me. In a split second I decided that this was it. This was where my life would end. I felt the pain of losing my son, the pain of him perhaps losing his life because of my own stupidity. I felt resignation. Guilt. Shame. Helplessness. Despair … I stopped moving my arms. I stopped kicking my feet. I let go of the sunglasses I was clinging to in my left hand and everything started moving in slow motion. I let go in a way I never had before. Terror. Raw pain. Blackness. Acceptance. Peace. Emptiness. Everything stood still as I fully surrendered and simply gave up. It seemed like the moment froze before me …

In that instant, a hand broke through the water's surface and dragged me up, pulling me out of the water to safety. A stranger who was passing by had reached into the pool to get me out. Shaking with shock I held on to him and wept.

"You saved my life," I told him. "Thank you!"

He smiled. His name was Andrew. How could it be? Not only the first name of my son but also the name of my uncle who had drowned in the ocean in Spain years before this day. My own Andrew, my AJ, was standing on the cliff above the natural pool watching me. I cried harder. He was okay! Relief. More tears. Contrary to what I thought when he was near me in the pool, he didn't have the same terrible experience as me. I hugged AJ tightly, still in a haze from the shock of it all.

In order to leave the area, we had to jump back into the natural pool to get back to the other side and hike back to the road. I was forced to jump back into the water that had almost taken my life. AJ went first. I closed my eyes and jumped in after him, scared shitless. Once on the other side, I was finally able to release what had just happened and I broke down completely, sobbing while AJ held me. *He* held *me*. It was such a significant moment of knowing that both of my children were now adults capable not just of taking care of themselves, but also holding *me* when and if I needed it. It was time to let go of the way I had been mothering and loving them up until this moment. Everything was evolving and shifting, including *love*. Love was asking to expand, or rather my idea of it.

*What is love?* I wondered. *Can I release everything I think love to be? Is that also blinding me from seeing what love actually is? Something much, much bigger ... My limited belief about what love is based on what I have experienced in life (the past informing the future). What if there is more to love?*

AJ and I made it back to the villa with the sign "THE UNKNOWN" on its living room wall. The name of the villa was UTOPIC, and I share this with you because the word "utopić" in Polish means "to drown." I shit you not. Once you start looking for meaning and symbolism in everything, all of life becomes a spiritual journey. Everything is sacred.

"I came here to drown," I said to myself, wondering how many times more I would come to St. Barths to die—to die and be reborn anew. This place transformed me every time. My soul came alive here and demanded she be released. Relentless, she didn't take "no" for an answer.

---

Back in Sarasota and again in confinement, it seemed like the whole world was moving online during the Covid pandemic. This allowed me access to all kinds of courses, masterclasses, and workshops and I took full advantage of them. I learned about contemplation and the gene keys, our energetic field and the energy/chakra system, the quantum field, rewiring the brain, reprogramming conditioning and old beliefs, manifesting and mindset work. I was always reading up on new developments in healing trauma, studying regulation of the nervous system, and practicing bringing safety to the body. I continued my morning ritual practice and journaling and living slow and with intention. The money I made from the sale of CheapCaribbean allowed for this to be my full-time work, not just my own healing but my desire to help others. I was determined. I knew it was a massive gift and I took the responsibility that came with it seriously. What could I learn, how much could I grow, so that I could then share this with those also suffering? I would become the experiment so that I could bring the hope I so much needed at the worst of my own struggles. I felt this would somehow give meaning and purpose to all my pain and trauma. Of course life gave me no choice in the matter so while it might sound admirable and courageous, most of the time it felt like the only way out of feeling like shit. I took it.

I invested in an emotional intelligence and somatic coach, a mind-body maturation mentor, and a quantum energetics and mindset coach, believing that surrounding myself with women who are already shining their light brightly would only lead the way for me. We continued breaking down my patterns and conditioning, as well as expanding my ability to sit with discomfort and shift my perspective (the story I was telling myself about what was happening). The goal was still to feel everything as it came up, in order to experience it, release it, and learn the lessons it brought. Panic attacks slowly ceased. Anxiety still came, but it wasn't something I avoided like a plague anymore. I got curious about it instead and welcomed it with compassion. Anxiety became a signal from my body's own wisdom that I needed to slow down—something was too much and I needed to pause and soothe. I started to simply trust that and go into my practice to address it. My capacity for sitting with my anxiety expanded. This is called the "window of tolerance" in trauma, and healing allows us to slowly and gently tolerate more and more discomfort. Not in a way that is harmful or "pushing through it" but in a kind, loving way that builds resilience. Some stress is actually healthy and perfectly normal for our brains and bodies, just not a constant onslaught of it. This is what growth looks like—expanding to hold more of our life experience—in a gentle and safe way. Anxiety sometimes brought me a message like "you're doing something out of obligation again" or "something about this doesn't feel good and you just ignored that, abandoning your needs again" or "you said yes when you really meant no" or "is it true that this is anxiety, or perhaps is it actually excitement?" It was truly a genius warning signal from my own body. Of course plenty of times, I just got lost in the fear of the experience, buckled under the sensations, and got taken over by the drama. I experienced plenty of failure. But I would keep trying. Triggers also became opportunities to heal and grow, even if they were still extremely hard. Instead of being mad and angry at the person who "triggered me," I started looking inside of myself. What was it, that was already inside of me that was being triggered? Why was my reaction so big to something so seemingly small? Again, plenty of times I would just explode in anger instead, and I am sharing that with you to be transparent and to give you plenty of permission to screw up. The goal isn't perfection but slow progress and loads of compassion. Simple awareness that there is another way is a huge step in the right direction. Again, my practice allowed me to pause and investigate rather than react. It allowed me to get to know myself more and to understand what was actually going on. I often journalled about the experience to myself and why I am the way I am. Then I could share this new insight with my husband, for example, and he would get to know me in a new way (rather than get in a huge fight). This kind of inner work really allowed for much deeper connection with other people because my connection to myself was getting really strong and authentic. I was learning intimacy.

The hard thing about this phase was letting old friendships

go, the surface friendships or the obligatory ones (you know the ones where you go to dinner and smile awkwardly the whole time while your insides just want to pick up your purse and run out the door barefoot). This too was making space for the new (release to receive). The important thing about this was not telling myself the story that I am alone, have no friends, and nobody gets me. But I did it anyway and then I felt sorry for myself, and when that moved through me, I just came back to the process. It was sort of like allowing the toddler within to have a fit, seeing her, validating her, honoring her pain, and then being the parent and taking charge saying, "Okay, that's good. Excellent work. That's enough. Now that that's out of your system, back to life." No drama. Not wallowing in victimhood but allowing the space to feel that's valid (anything you feel is valid! It's just not supposed to linger or create drama). This is what healing looks like. This is growth. This is the spiritual path. It is messy. It is never a straight line upward. It doesn't even feel like forward movement a lot of the time. But it is this trusting that everything, every little experience and event in life, has a purpose. There is always something to learn from it. Oftentimes, that was the last freaking thing I wanted to hear! That's why it is equally important to create time to play and have fun.

Time also came to start living into this new identity I was uncovering. Once again, I knew I needed guidance. Rather than competing and comparing, which would result in guilt and shame (thanks social media!), I decided to encircle myself with soul sisters already doing the work I envisioned myself doing, knowing that just being in their field of energy, I was elevating my own vibration.

*Want to make changes in your life? Surround yourself with people doing things differently already*, I thought, *rather than complaining about what sucks and is not working.* I also read somewhere that we are a combination of the five people we spend the most time with, so I paid attention to who was in my inner circle. (Who is in yours?) This led to a two-year journey of more processing, releasing, and unbecoming. I was healing, growing, and expanding exponentially. This was the period of my biggest transformation.

My mentors and coaches were great at pulling back the veils on blind spots I could not access myself. They also guided me to reconnect to fun, lightness, pleasure, and play in my life—asking what made me come alive inside and what made the little girl in me giddy with joy. This was the new foundation for rebuilding the new life I was preparing to begin. Asking my heart what made it happy was connecting to my true self. I wanted to live out of this space versus the rules and obligations and logic that drove my life's decisions previously.

I wanted lightness and delight after what seemed like years and years of hard work, of hanging out in the dark spaces and shadows, and doing the heavy lifting. I wanted to play, dance, dream, and envision the next season of my life. "Radical receiving" became my theme and I started opening my heart even more to what was available to me from this space of feeling good inside. What could I create if I came to life already fulfilled, happy, at peace, and loved? What if I didn't need any of that to come from outside of myself—from the people around me, the external circumstances, the jobs I held, the things I did? Could I feel so connected to my own soul that I showed up everywhere already full, already abundant and overflowing with love, looking at everything else in life as just the cherry on top of something already amazing? What if there wasn't this desperate need for all those things, circumstances, and people to be just right in order for me to feel okay? What if my externals were simply a direct reflection of my internal state, and the answer to everything I had been seeking was simply this: go to the root, heal the wounds deep in my heart, address the problem at its core and watch everything else fall into place. What if all of life is an inside-out process and we just have been taught to focus on the wrong thing all along?

———————

I knew I was finally coming home—home to myself. This inner journey was a path leading from the mind to the heart. It is such a short distance in the physical realm but a road not traveled by many and one that takes the longest time to complete. This was where I ultimately found what I had been seeking: belonging and freedom. It was within me all along. I was the "home" I had been longing for since immigration, since childhood, and perhaps even since birth. Within me was the freedom I had been searching for— the quest my ancestors and generations before me completed. The kind of freedom and belonging that can never be taken away because they aren't dependent on external circumstances. I was always already free and I was always already home. I just couldn't see it with all the layers I had accumulated during my life—they hid this fact from me. What started as healing, turned into self-discovery, and became a spiritual quest, was a journey of returning to and remembering what had been within me all along: home, freedom, love, and belonging. Everything I had been seeking.

Underneath it all—underneath the story of who I thought I was, everything I was doing, and everything that happened to me—I found my heart. She reminded me of my purpose. My heart reminded me of who I really am and why I am here. I am a presence of love. I am a presence of love whose source is a pure Love— holy, sacred, unlimited, and infinite. This Love, this Divine Force, orchestrates everything in life and pours itself into me, merging with my spirit. At my core is an endless waterfall of love, which never runs out and never ends and always overflows. This is my very essence, this abundance.

———————

I am sacred and whole and I am here to connect you to your heart, while holding you in this presence of love. I am here to guide you in caring for your soul and nourishing your spirit. I myself don't have the answers you are seeking, but I help you to remember that you already know. You just need to slow down and go within. It is radically simple and truly profound. You too are pure love at your core; once you experience it, you will end desperately seeking it outside of yourself. Think of the powerful impact that could have on your life. What you are longing for is within you. You already have "that thing" you think you're lacking; you just can't see it. This is the secret that allows you to get off the roller coaster of life and living stuck in cycles and patterns. Start living from the truth of who you really are—your soul—which is whole, sacred, and wonderfully, beautifully unique. That's incredibly powerful—and completely available to you. You just need to choose it over the distractions of the external world. Choose yourself. See your own worthiness and decide to pour into your own heart as you have poured out into others. Love yourself enough to stop looking for love in other people.

Freedom for me started the moment I was able to define what held me captive, once I could see where I thought I was unfree. But before the truth could set me free, I needed to see what lies held me prisoner and to believe that I actually held the keys to my own jail cell. The journey began by letting myself completely unravel, come undone, come unglued, fall apart. This was the start that was prompted by the feeling that something just wasn't right. Something was off. There was more to life. There was more to me. And the questions. All the questions: "What am I doing here?" "What is my purpose?" "What is the point of all this?" "Who even am I?" Allowing these to linger with no answer started me on my journey.

Now I simply continue the letting go and unbecoming. A little bit more each day! I consciously choose the rules I want to live by and no longer accept handed-down expectations and roles I "should" play. This is freedom. I cocreate the life I want to live by setting boundaries and making choices that serve me and my well-being and then allowing myself to be led to the next thing. I release the stories that hold me prisoner—about being different, about being a stranger, about needing to change that, about being broken. Instead I embrace what makes me truly me and try to bring that forth and let my light shine to make way for others so they can shine theirs. A lighthouse shining love out her windows. I live with the intention of fully expressing myself authentically and to do that, I must know myself. So I continue peeling back the petals of the rose and letting old beliefs that no longer serve me die, letting old versions of myself that I've outgrown die, letting the ways I limit myself dissolve. I am constantly in a state of letting go and changing, which can still be hard because I've been hanging on to things for dear life for so long!

However, the releasing creates space for the new, for the unknown, which I now welcome with curiosity. I am constantly evolving. I allow life to unfold before me and I trust that it is all working out *for* me. This brings magic into my life—coincidences, synchronicities, miracles, and surprises. I expect to encounter them now, rather than disaster and danger. This also brings authentic friendships and soul companions my way. Because I am being authentically me, the people who are meant to be in my life can now more easily find me because they can recognize me without my masks. I know I am not for everyone, and that's okay.

By staying true to my heart—not repressing, not pretending, not becoming, not perfecting or performing—I have stopped attracting the surface friendships and the relationships that were always a one-way dynamic based on my wounding. My marriage is stronger than ever, as is the bond with my children and the love for my parents, sister and family. With each small step I take back my power a little bit more; I come home a little more; I claim my own freedom a little more. Each day I discover a new part of my soul, my true self emerges more fully, and each day I love her more deeply and take radical responsibility for her evolution, maturation, and expansion. Most of all, I stay connected to my soul and live my life with a fully open heart. And when I forget and get lost in pain, the difficulty of life, the suffering that takes place here, the darkness that wants to swallow me whole, I surround myself with people who can remind me of who I am.

It is true! I can do anything and I can be anyone. And today I simply choose to be love—everywhere and to everyone—because for me it all comes down to love. Radical love. Love for others and for love for myself. Love for my screwups and mistakes, when I unintentionally hurt other people and pick the wrong thing for myself or fall into an old pattern. We are human. The intent is never perfection.

I hope that by sharing the story of my deepest wounds, pain, and trauma, you can know that we all have those experiences. I ask that you hold my wide-open heart tenderly as you read these pages because it is a vulnerable place to be, standing so naked before the world. But I want you to know that your wounds, pain, and trauma are valid and real simply by showing you all of mine. However, they need not hold you hostage. They need not isolate you. This is how I alchemized my suffering to be of service to others—and this is my gift to you—to give you hope and a promise that you can do the same. Perhaps even offer you some tips on how to get started. Because my story is somehow your story. Your pain and suffering are my pain and suffering. My healing is your healing. Your freedom is my freedom … We are all connected. We are all one. We are all this love I am learning to tap into and be. May my own journey offer a lamp to your feet while you walk toward your own liberation. It already awaits you within. Do you dare to claim it for yourself? You can do anything. You can be anyone. I believe in you. I hope you believe in yourself. Slow down and break open in order to break through and then break free. I'll be there to hold you through it. You got this.

With love and compassion, from my soul to yours,

Marta

# CHAPTER 12

# Soulcare Practice

There is an ancient part of you within, called your soul. We get so focused on the externals, the goals, the stuff, the plans, and all the forcing and striving it takes to get there. We push ourselves and forget to tune in, to ask how all this actually feels. We ignore the soul and her wisdom. This was my story of how I started listening and how I reconnected. This is the journey, my search, my path toward my own heart—to my true self, my essence, the real *me*. The soul is always communicating. I had ignored her for so long that a crisis was needed to get my attention. But if you're experiencing the gentle knockings, the whispers, the invitations—listen. They may come as anxiety, panic attacks, insomnia, a feeling of something being off, a lostness or confusion, wondering if you're in the right job or the right relationship or the right city ... They may come as questions like "Who am I?" or "What is my purpose" or "What am I even doing here?!" These are all gifts ... slow down and notice them. Don't fear them. Don't run from them any longer by staying busy. Simply place one hand on your heart, bring your attention to your breath, close your eyes so you can see more, and listen. What is the message you are meant to hear? Let the thoughts come and go trying to scream for your attention—stay with the breath. Just for five minutes each morning to start the day, be *with* yourself and *slow down*. For a moment, feel the experience of being *you* in the body, not in the mind. Feel your aliveness. What does your heart want you to know? This is how you too can begin to meet yourself ...

I wanted to leave you with some tools and practical steps on how you can begin your own inner journey—slowing down, getting quiet, connecting to your heart, and nourishing your soul. Please find below a practice I've developed called SoulCare, which is what I use, after the many years of healing, seeking, learning, researching, and experimenting, which I described in this book. I hope you find it as helpful as I do.

It starts with *safety*. Slowing down without downshifting gently can be triggering (even traumatizing), so it is important to fully arrive in the present moment, in the space you're in, and in your body.

Once your nervous system feels safe (this is not a thinking-brain thing—you have to signal to your body that it is okay to come out of flight-flight-freeze-fawn mode, and I describe for you how to do this), the second thing to remember is *wholeness*. This means that when you sit down for this practice, you allow anything and everything to come up. The parts of yourself or emotions you have been trying to repress or hide are all welcome. We are trying to move from fragmentation to integration—all of you is welcome! No need to be a certain way, no need to hide anything, just be fully you. All of you. If anger, sadness, grief, loneliness, or intense joy, peace, or contentment come, welcome them. Whatever comes through you, allow it. Feel it all in your heart.

The third and last thing I want you to remember is *love*. Do not judge the thoughts, feelings, emotions, sensations. Do not label them or make up a story or narrative to go with them. Do not make them mean anything about who you are. Do not call them "good" or "bad," and do not feel guilty or ashamed for feeling anything that arises. Welcome it with love and hold it with love.

Breathe through it knowing that it is going slow and going

gentle that begins the healing that leads to an intimate connection with yourself—your own inner journey and path toward your soul and your spirit. The way forward is through the heart and in order to move toward your soul, you have to feel anything and everything in your heart. Witness it all and remember that you are not the feelings, thoughts, or emotions you are experiencing. You are the one who is feeling, thinking, and experiencing them. Hold yourself through the practice with tenderness and love. Drape a warm blanket or a soft scarf over your shoulders if it helps you to feel the holding. Get cozy.

If you can stay focused on your breathing, whatever comes up to be felt and acknowledged will eventually pass. You will have successfully released the stuck energy that simply needed releasing. And you will have opened up your heart a little bit more each time you allow yourself to feel. No need to overthink this. Just let things that have been stuck inside go. Let them come and let them go. Let them move through you. Let them move you. Exhale deeply and completely.

Underneath all that, you will encounter a moment of pure stillness and solitude. It might be just a second at first, but it will eventually lengthen. This is the space of true connection to yourself, to your soul. Allow yourself to experience it fully—opening your heart to it—drinking in the calm and peace. Simply imagining your heart opening will mean your heart is opening. Simply noticing the calm and peace and lingering in it rather than rushing out of it allows you to experience it fully. When you are ready, you will give thanks, open your eyes, and move on with your day. You only need ten minutes to start. Here is how:

1.  Set aside ten minutes of uninterrupted time in a quiet place. Sit comfortably on a flat surface: chair, sofa, bed, or floor. How you sit is unimportant; just make sure that your back

is straight so that your spine is tall. Take a full body stretch, shrug your shoulders up and down, twist to each side a few times, and bring each cheek to each shoulder, one then the other. Turn your head left and right, nod up and down, and get comfortable in your seat.

2.   Mentally, set the intention to leave your schedule, to do list, and agenda aside—just for these next ten minutes. They will be there for you to get back to. Check everything else outside the door—hit the pause button on life. You can do it. Visualize leaving it all outside of the room you are in, as if you were putting it aside in a suitcase and shutting it away. Just for now. Feel the relief of this. Exhale.

3.   Start by using your five senses to orientate yourself in your surroundings. What can you see around you? What can you smell? What can you hear? What can you touch? What can you taste? Use this quick exercise in order to fully arrive in the space you are occupying.

4.   If it feels safe for you to do so, close your eyes. If it makes you uncomfortable, simply focus your gaze on an object in front of you or lower your gaze to the floor, softening your focus.

5.   Starting at the bottom of your feet, use your imagination to do a body scan. Just begin focusing your attention on one body part at a time, noticing tension, asking each body part to relax and rest. Move your awareness up from the feet all the way to the top of your head. Use this step to fully arrive in your body.

6.   Now focus on your breath. Find a place in your body where you can really feel the breath moving you, noticing how your body is breathing you. Perhaps you can notice your chest rising up and down or your belly moving in and out or maybe you feel the cool air move through your nostrils or in your throat.

Don't change how you are breathing. Just notice the breath. Do this for a couple of minutes. This step starts the process of shifting from the external experience to the internal—going within.

7. Whenever you are ready, start moving into conscious breathing, where you will begin to manipulate the breath. It isn't difficult. Simply inhale through your nose for a count of 4 and exhale through your mouth for a count of 6. The longer exhales send a signal to your nervous system and your brain that you are safe. This is a great exercise to switch off your fight-or-flight mode, which we are used to living out of most of the time. Do this for three rounds of six breaths, keeping the eyes closed (or the gaze low).

8. Let go of the controlled breathing and place one hand on your heart. Notice the stillness, silence, and solitude around you. Notice the peace you just cultivated. From this place of calm and inner peace, ask your heart if it has something to tell you. Ask your soul if it has a message for you. Sit here for a long moment and listen and be still. If thoughts come (and they will), find the breath again. This is where emotions will come up if you allow them. Let yourself experience whatever it might be, knowing that it is only looking to be acknowledged, felt, and released. You are simply honoring whatever wants to come up and be seen and held. Come back to your breath if the emotions get overwhelming. Keep the hand on your heart as a reminder of you holding yourself with love through this. You are not by yourself. You are with yourself. Once the energy of the emotion releases, the stillness will come. Take a couple of deep breaths here and just experience it. Simply be and listen here. Breathe. Remember gentleness, tenderness, and love—imagine your heart opening wide with love for yourself. Don't rush this. Stay here for as long as it feels good.

9.   Whether or not you hear or see anything, take a moment to give thanks. Feeling your own palm on your own heart space, express your gratitude in whatever way feels right to you. Sometimes we have to come back to clearing the stuff blocking us from seeing or hearing guidance repeatedly. Do not be discouraged. Commit to yourself and commit to the practice for it to bear fruit.

10.  Slowly place your hand back down. Pause. Take a deep inhale and a complete exhale. Do this two more times. Now wiggle your fingers and your toes. Shrug your shoulders and turn your neck to each side in a way that feels good. Take a full body stretch. Smile. :) Whenever you are ready, and not a moment before, gently blink open your eyes.

11.  If you have time, now is the perfect opportunity to journal about the experience. Often insight comes after we have had time for everything to integrate. Write down everything, knowing that what you don't understand right away will make sense later. It is also a good idea to journal so that you don't forget what happened as your day and life pull you back into their busy pace. Coming back to these moments in your journal will keep them alive in your mind and encourage you to continue showing up for yourself. Pay attention to any dreams, experiences, gut feelings, hints, or strange coincidences later in your day. They are important. Journal about those as well. Reflect on them. Ask why.

12.  You are now ready to move back into your day. Slowly. Can you bring the calm you experienced during this practice with you as you go? Can you show up amid the everyday chaos as the grounded, calm one with a sense of peace about you? Even if just for a moment here and there? Try it.

Remember this space within you is available for you anytime you need it. Come back to it often. Slow down as many times in your day as you can, even if only to pause, take a deep breath, and feel your feet on the ground beneath you. You strengthen your relationship with your soul by practicing communicating with it and by connecting to your heart. Try to do a short version of this practice before going to bed, if you started your day with it in the morning (which is what I recommend). You can visit www. MartaHobbs.com/unraveling for an audio version of it as well as the full SoulCare practice I teach in person.

Slow down…

Tune in.

Listen. Be. Breathe.

Everything you long for awaits you within.

Take the path inward and awaken to your beautiful heart.

Connect to your soul. Meet your true self.

You are sacred. You are whole. You are love.

And so it is.

# Acknowledgments:

## My Deepest Love And Gratitude

First and foremost, to my parents, who gave me life, provided me with a home and taught me love, family and belonging. Thank you for loving me deeply, teaching me to fight for my freedom and reminding me that I can do anything. Thank you for bringing me to America, as hard as it was for us all. I am extremely grateful for the beautiful life this traumatic event provided. Kocham Was.

Thank you to my sister Ania for being my companion, often my only one, through the dark and scary times in our lives as young girls and young women. I love you and am so proud of who you are today. I wrote a lot of this with you in mind, as you began your own healing journey. Even though it will look different than mine, may my story encourage you to keep going and know that you are always loved. You will find your own path. Trust that. I love you.

To my husband Jim for being so supportive and open as I exposed some of our deepest pains and biggest heartbreaks. Thank you for the journey we have been on together and the growth and healing which is only possible in a sacred partnership, which our marriage has become. It has been an amazing ride! While the highs were high, and lows were low, I am so thankful we have found a space in between filled with safety, peace, tenderness and a deep, deep love. I am excited about what we are cocreating in this next season of our life together. I love you. Thank you for seeing me and loving me.

To my children, Mira and AJ, whom I dedicate this book to —
thank you for teaching me the kind of love I didn't know existed
before you came into my life. Thank you for the treasure of getting
to guide you and watch you bloom. Thank you for being my
mirrors and helping me see places in myself that needed healing.
You are both incredible and I am so proud of the amazing human
beings you are. In my healing, at its hardest and most terrifying
moments, it was you, your two hearts, that kept me going. Thank
you for providing me the strength to put one foot in front of the
other, when I thought I could not. I hope this book not only allows
you to see me as the person I am outside of being your mama, I
hope the work it describes lifts the heavy burden of trauma that
has been carried by our lineage off your shoulders. I hope it frees
you and shows you that anything is possible for you both, which
I have always told you. I hope you too remember your sacredness
and how very loved you are. Go out there and pave your own path -
shine your light and share your gifts. You are absolute miracles and
I love and cherish you.

I started writing this book in order to heal. It began as journal
entries, poems of anger and bullet points of grief on paper soaked
in the rivers of my tears - expressing the feelings I wasn't able to
voice for most of my life. I did not think of it as a book, but a
cathartic process to free myself from my trauma.

It was with the encouragement and support of some amazing
people who entered my life just at the right moment that the idea
of publishing began. When I thought back, I remembered that I
had been hearing "You should write a book!" very often – as often
as I was willing to share my full story, which wasn't that frequently
in the past. As I started to hear this whisper in 2018, I realized that
it was a familiar invitation. Rather than follow the logical path of
pursuing my master's degree in Mental Health Counseling at New
York University, where I had just been accepted, I wrote instead.

I followed the calling of my soul. I followed my heart and not my mind. I did the thing that didn't make sense and presented me with a huge risk – exposing my deepest wounds to complete strangers. Filled with fear, I took a plunge into the unknown. And so, this book became my purpose for three years – through Covid and the difficult journey I describe in the second part of "Unraveling." And now as I release it into the world my only hope is that it helps others like me who feel so alone and lost. My deepest gratitude to the following souls, without whom this book would not be here today:

Debbie Kadagian – thank you for echoing the calling of my soul in a way that I could not miss it this time. Thank you for your therapy sessions during the hardest times, for your friendship, love and reading my first drafts.

Katie Pearson – thank you for coaching insights, wisdom and asking the right questions at the right time. Thank you for the birth of the big dream to make this into a movie and what it awakened within me.

Odette Lockwood-Stewart – thank you for your spiritual direction, love, support and deeply rooted soul-sisterhood while on this journey (and always). I love you.

Diana Bourel – thank you for teaching me about yoga, breath and physically picking me up off the floor when I thought the terror and grief would kill me. I have cried in your embrace more times than I can count. Thank you for teaching me to keep my heart open during the hard times. Thank you for your deep, deep love and safe holding. I love you.

Michael Cusick – thank you for holding me through the hardest two weeks of my life. Thank you for the faith you always had in me to come out on the other side. Thank you for reminding me that I will be the one to write the book I was looking for while healing my trauma. Thank you for being the first to hold my entire story and make me feel seen.

Nicky Clinch – thank you for the profound healing of our work together and the deepest part of my transformation. Thank you for planting the seed of "freedom" and your mentorship while I figured out what exactly I wanted to write and at the times where I was sure I should quit. Thank you for guiding me home. I love you.

Anna Zweede – thank you for coming back into my life in perfectly divine timing – just when I was ready to give up on this project. You breathed new life into it and co-creating it with you was one of the biggest gifts to me. Thank you for this partnership. I love you.

Suzy Ashworth – thank you for constantly reminding me that I am sacred, divine and limitless. Thank you for loving me when I would forget. Thank you for the permission I so needed to live out of the space of abundance and expecting miracles. Thank you for your enthusiasm, soul-nourishing friendship and love. I cherish you.

Shannon Kaiser – thank you for your crucial work in pushing this labor of love across the finish line. I could not have done it without you. Your guidance, love and faith in me were just what I needed to complete and release this baby into the world.

To the therapists, healers, coaches and teachers who held me during my journey: Anne Belgram-Perkins, Jennifer Vollrath Dimitriou, Philippe Wuyts, Max Strom, Joo Chye Teoh, Heather Leah Boreske, Deanine Picciano, Claudia Baeza, Tiana Dillard, Gemma Gambee Lewis, Paul Chubbuck, Elisa White and Nanda Mortier, Valerie Oula, Courtni Gafken Allison. Thank you all so much.

Thank you, Alexis Gargagliano, Danielle Brock, Nikki Van De Car, Caroline Dahlmanns, Rachel Calvo, Christina Thiele for your invaluable creative contributions to this labor of love. Thank you, Brianne Bardusch, for your detailed, tender and loving editing of my manuscript.

To my friends who supported and loved me during the times I describe in this book – from New York, to Pennsylvania, Paris, London, St Barths and Sarasota – thank you. I love you.

To you, my dear reader… my biggest thanks. I have spent hours in meditation visualizing you reading my story and recognizing yourself in parts of it. I hope it touches your heart deeply and makes you feel less alone in whatever you are going through or have been through in the past. My biggest dream and desire is that in my unraveling you find hope and courage for your own healing and transformation. It is an amazing journey – may it lead you home.

With all my love,

Marta

# About the Author

Marta Hobbs was born in Szczecin, Poland and immigrated to the United States at the age of 12, fleeing the Communist oppression of her homeland as a political refugee with her parents, younger sister and their dog. The challenges of immigration to and assimilation in the USA left Marta with deep scars and pushed her to relentlessly pursue "the American Dream." After a decade-long successful career in TV Production in New York City, Marta co-founded CheapCaribbean.com, with her husband Jim.

At 38, after a move to Paris, France and a highly successful sale of the company, Marta experienced a personal crisis brought on by sudden onset of panic attacks, paralyzing anxiety and terrifying health issues. This unraveling sparked a healing journey into holistic wellness including yoga, meditation, breathwork, nutrition, stress management, trauma recovery, various types of therapy, somatic and energetic work as well as over a decade of personal development and inner work. This spiritual walk brought forth an awakening of insight, wisdom, and a desire to help others navigate the challenges she herself had faced and overcome.

As the founder and teacher of SoulCare – a spiritual practice to slow down the body, quiet the mind and reconnect with the soul – Marta now guides others toward healing, self-discovery and living a heart-centered and soul-led life. She also mentors and accompanies powerful leaders who find themselves overwhelmed and lonely in their roles, as well as curates and designs holistic wellness programs for corporations focused on heart-connection, soul-care and leading from within. Marta believes that the answers to everything we seek in life are within each one of us and our external life is simply a reflection of our internal state. We are sacred and whole at our core; we have just forgotten this truth. Therefore, finding lasting happiness, love, health, fulfillment and purpose in life is a process of remembering as well as an inside-out job.

To learn about working with Marta, or to inquire about booking her for your next event visit www.MartaHobbs.com.

Printed in Great Britain
by Amazon

19428554R00149